DEVOTIONS®

September

I will sing to the LORD all my life; I will sing praise to my God as long as I live.

—*Psalm 104:33*

Gary Wilde, Editor   **Margaret Williams,** Project Editor   Photo © Kmitu | Dreamstime.com

DEVOTIONS® is published quarterly by Standard Publishing, Cincinnati, Ohio, www.standardpub.com. © 2012 by Standard Publishing. All rights reserved. Topics based on the Home Daily Bible Readings, International Sunday School Lessons. © 2010 by the Committee on the Uniform Series. Printed in the U.S.A. All Scripture quotations, unless otherwise indicated, are taken from the *HOLY BIBLE, NEW INTERNATIONAL VERSION®. NIV®.* Copyright © 2011 by Biblica, Inc.™ Used by permission of Zondervan. All rights reserved. The *New American Standard Bible®* (*NASB*). Copyright © 1960, 1962, 1963, 1968, 1971, 1972, 1973, 1975, 1977, 1995 by The Lockman Foundation. Used by permission. (www.Lockman.org). All rights reserved. The Holy Bible, *New Living Translation* (*NLT*). Copyright © 1996, 2004. Used by permission of Tyndale House Publishers, Inc., Wheaton, Illinois 60189. All rights reserved. *The Contemporary English Version* (*CEV*) Copyright © 1991, 1992, 1995 by American Bible Society. Used by permission. All rights reserved..

Dinner Time

All creatures look to you to give them their food at the proper time (Psalm 104:27).

Scripture: Psalm 104:5-9, 24-30
Song: "God Sees the Little Sparrow Fall"

Five o'clock is dinner time, and my dog, Santana, knows it. Whether he's outside or waiting by his dish, he's always eager to chow down. He comes running at full speed into the kitchen as soon as he hears food hitting the bowl and waits until I give him the OK to eat. He isn't picky. He is finished by the time I get back to my living room, and he is satisfied.

Psalm 104 describes how creation works. As Santana looks to me for food and care, the entire creation looks to God to take care of its needs. That's how He made it. In His wisdom, God designed the fish in the sea, the birds of the air, and other living things to roam the earth. He saw to it that every creature had the proper environment to live in, complete with food to eat and water to drink.

The Lord is truly masterful in administering His creation! Look around today and see how great our God is. Listen to the birds and hear their praise for life. Feel the wind and be reminded that the Spirit of God is near. Be aware of His creation today and know that you too are in His care.

Lord, how wonderful is Your work! As I go about my day, help me to remember that You take care of all of Your creation with perfect and infinite care—including me. All praise to You, through Christ my Lord. Amen.

September 1. **Tait Berge** is the church relations director at Mephibosheth Ministry. He lives in Colorado Springs and, when not working, enjoys hockey and golf.

Order Out of Chaos

God made . . . all the creatures . . . And God saw that it was good (Genesis 1:25).

Scripture: Genesis 1:20-25
Song: "Be Still and Know"

I glanced at my watch as I slid behind the wheel. As the minutes fled, I realized Tiffany waited at school and was late for her rehearsal. Furthermore, I had missed Troy's game—and choir practice was in one hour! Disorder blew around me like confetti in the wind. How could I escape this chaos? Was this hectic pace really God's plan for my life?

This morning I watch the quaking aspen tree outside my window; its leaves flash as they quiver in the still air. An industrious robin tends her brood. At this moment, I know God is the author of order. He divided chaos into night and day and separated animals into categories, each category their own kind. In God's plan, life became organized and structured. He set a system in place and saw that it was good.

When I choose too many activities to fill a single day, I introduce chaos. My mind shuts down, and only "erratic flight" characterizes my thinking processes. But I can decide to go to God—and this time stay long enough to listen. He changes the tempo and brings order when I let Him create my day.

O God, author of peace, I know You wait patiently for me every day, but I so often run past You. Create structure for me and give me a quiet heart that seeks You first. Thank You, through Christ my Savior. Amen.

September 2–8. **Barbara Durnil** is a retired medical worker and freelance writer in Southern Idaho. Writing for God is her joy and passion.

Marvelously Made

God saw all that He had made, and behold, it was very good. And there was evening and there was morning, the sixth day (Genesis 1:31, *New American Standard Bible*).

Scripture: Genesis 1:26-31
Song: "I Am Loved"

I drove away from the luncheon feeling depressed. Sharon had it all. Her physical perfection radiated with blinding annoyance. She had a loving husband and two darling children. Their classic two-story home stood in an upscale neighborhood and included a pool off the patio, with a BMW in the driveway.

What had happened to me? I lived alone, drove an old Ford truck, and every day was a bad-hair-day. My self-esteem hit the floor with a sorry thud.

"Why so downcast, O my soul?" What's that you say? The words repeat themselves in my mind. I remember that God is my Creator, and He has set me apart from all creation as a unique personality. God made me in His image.

Here's a thought: If I begin to measure myself by human standards, isn't it degrading to the Lord himself? After all, I reflect God's character through the Holy Spirit in me. Possessions and money matter not to God. It is my life in Him that carries infinite value. As I put my hope in God and praise Him, my self-worth comes into perspective. When I see my life through His eyes—behold, it is very good.

Creator God, open my heart that I may know how precious I am to You. When I realize Your love for me, useless comparisons leave me. Your hand formed me, and Your breath gives me life. In You, I find my worth. Through Christ, amen.

It Is Finished

By the seventh day God completed His work which He had done, and He rested on the seventh day from all His work which He had done (Genesis 2:2, *New American Standard Bible*).

Scripture: Genesis 2:1-9
Song: "I Heard the Voice of Jesus Say"

Ouch! My pinched finger throbbed as I dropped the steel fence post into the truck. I turned for the roll of wire, and my back complained as I heaved its weight up to the tailgate. I really disliked building a fence! It was exhausting. The road ended at the trees, and I gathered a load of posts. But beyond the big cedar, I stopped short.

What in the world was that? There on the line stood a new wire fence. The completed work glistened through the trees, and I had not driven a single one of those posts. I plucked the taught wire and tested the rock-solid posts. The work was perfect, and I could rest.

A breeze touched my face as I sank to the forest floor. This gift lifted my heart, and my body relaxed. *What a great neighbor I have!*

In the same way, God gives me rest from my work to earn His favor. He himself rested, not from fatigue, but because He finished creation. He asks me to rest now in the completion of His redemptive work. There is no labor needed to improve *that* gift or to make it mine, other than trust Him and accept His grace.

Father, my salvation is complete because the work of Jesus on the cross is finished for eternity. I now put my energy into trusting You, instead of trusting my efforts to earn Your favor. Hold me now, as I rest in Your arms. In Jesus' name, amen.

See That Special Image

When Adam had lived one hundred and thirty years, he became the father of a son in his own likeness, according to his image, and named him Seth (Genesis 5:3, *New American Standard Bible*).

Scripture: Genesis 5:1-5
Song: "I Love You with the Love of the Lord"

"Whose child are you, and where did you come from?" Have you ever heard that from a frustrated parent? I have said it myself a few times. Then there is the standard, "You get that from your father." Inherited traits range from curly hair to athletic prowess; some are negative, many positive. (So I tend to take *selective* credit for the various traits of my children.)

I wonder if Eve looked at Seth and saw Adam. She must have, for there were no grandparents to cloud the reflection of the child. As he grew, did he become the astonishing image of his father? Did he act and speak like Adam?

But wait—he was made in *whose* image? Adam was created in God's image, and Seth according to that image too. It seems that grandpa's nose doesn't matter so much, because it is God's image that is supremely important. When I forget the physical genetics and look for God revealed in my children—and in people around me—I begin to see great potential and purpose. It's the image of God in us that gives value and significance to every life.

O Creator God, the prophet Samuel saw the physical image of David, but You saw the heart and soul. Help me see my children and others with Your eyes—eyes that pierce the outer crust and see the value and potential that lies within. Amen.

Voice of Triumph

Through the praise of children and infants you have established a stronghold against your enemies, to silence the foe and the avenger (Psalm 8:2).

Scripture: Psalm 8
Song: "Clap Your Hands All You People"

"Mama, don't be sad, Jesus will take care of you. Look, see the flower, the stem is all bent over, but Jesus keeps the flower beautiful!" Her big blue eyes reflected the innocence of her heart. Absolute trust and open love for God hung in the air, and I gathered Jenna in my arms.

Her simple praise had broken my fear. That morning, when I received medical test results calling for a biopsy, a battle began. Cancer ran in my family—but I was too young for this attack! Fear instantly gripped me, and I began to plan my strategy for the months ahead. How quickly my prayers became bargains and pleas with personal motives and agendas attached. I lost my stronghold.

Children sing "Jesus Loves Me" because they know He does. There is no labor to earn it, no bargain to make; their praise bubbles up from simple honesty. And when I lay down my battle plans and pick up a childlike trust, then my praise becomes pure, and strongholds are set against the enemy. My praise becomes a shout to God with a voice of triumph.

Almighty God and Father, help me simply to know that You are my eternal stronghold. Strengthen my belief and unreserved trust in You so that my praise will be as pure and innocent as a child's. It is that praise that brings my victory. Through Christ, amen.

The Better Way

That you be renewed in the spirit of your mind, and put on the new self, which in the likeness of God has been created in righteousness and holiness of the truth (Ephesians 4:23, 24, *New American Standard Bible*).

Scripture: Ephesians 4:17-24
Song: "Create in Me a Clean Heart"

My feet hit the floor with new resolve. This was a new day, and I planned to change my attitude. I would greet each customer with a smile and a gracious spirit. And when the complaints and harsh words came at me, I would be compassionate and understanding.

I could do this. My determination was high . . . until the first stoplight . . . and the impatient driver behind me honked the instant the light turned green. At the store, a customer pushed past me as I unlocked the door. I checked my watch: it was four minutes before the hour, and my spirit took another dive. *O God, what is wrong with me? Why can't I love as you love?*

That, in fact, is the problem. I can't. My decision to do so doesn't make it happen. David cried, "God, give me a clean heart and steadfast spirit." He had it right, didn't he? God must give me a new heart and new spirit, or I will continue to struggle.

God doing the work, however, liberates me! I become free from my own effort and ultimate failure. I can indeed get up each morning and ask God to create the heart that will carry me through the day.

O God, thank You for freeing me from the labor, and the guilt, when I fail. Create Your heart in me today and renew my spirit with Yours. In the name of Jesus, I pray. Amen.

People Who Need People . . .

It is not good for the man to be alone. I will make a helper suitable for him (Genesis 2:18).

Scripture: Genesis 2:18-25
Song: "Bind Us Together"

I am a solitary person. When I have a choice, I avoid crowds and large parties. In fact, I've been known to remain in seclusion for days at a time, coming out only to forage for food.

Horses, dogs, and barnyard animals make great companions. I discovered several years after widowhood, however, that being a mild recluse just wasn't God's plan for me. As I "dug in" on my property and withdrew, it became apparent that it wasn't working. I needed someone to hold me responsible and to help me grow. I needed incentive and mental stimulation. I also needed to give part of myself to others. My animals were companions, but there was no kinship. I needed *people*.

God found no partner for Adam in animals; instead, He duplicated His image from Adam's flesh. God placed people together so they could uphold each other, which resulted in blessing.

The body of Christ is made up of people. That body stimulates love and good deeds and brings cheer by speaking the wonders of God. Need enrichment? Come before Him with thanks, speak to one another "through psalms, hymns, and songs from the Spirit, singing to God with gratitude in your hearts" (see Colossians 3:16).

Precious Lord, never let me grow complacent about my position in Your body. It is there I find support, and there that I offer support to others. Though You dwell in my heart, remind me that Your gifts are to be used in Your church. In Jesus' name, amen.

From Utah to . . . God

You yourselves have seen what I did to Egypt, and how I carried you on eagles' wings and brought you to myself (Exodus 19:4).

Scripture: Exodus 19:3-8
Song: "Keep on Praying"

Moving day, 4:30 a.m., and the house is empty except for the sleeping bag I lie in. With great excitement I anticipate my 17-hour drive from Utah to my new home in Colorado.

At dawn, while I was driving on a deserted mountain road, a large doe ran in front of my SUV. I was going too fast to just slam on the breaks. *Smash!*

I pulled the car off the road and cried hysterically. The front of the car was bent so the front right tire couldn't move, the radiator was cracked, and the deer was dead. And no one was around to help. All I could do was pray.

Soon, out of nowhere, a tow truck driver going home from his night shift arrived and pulled out the car's damaged bumper so I could drive. He explained that the car could still make it to Colorado.

In a desperate moment, God heard my prayer—I hadn't been in a church for years. Once settled into my new home, my neighbor invited me to dinner and then to church. God brought me from Utah back to Him.

Lord, thanks for being with me when scary things happen. Though I hadn't been close to You, You never left me. You heard my call for help. In Jesus' name, amen.

September 9–15. **Dee Martz** lives in Louisville, Colorado. She is an office manager, technical writer, and editor. She walks dogs for the Humane Society.

Obedient Blessings

See, I am setting before you today a blessing and a curse—the blessing if you obey the commands of the Lord your God that I am giving you today (Deuteronomy 11:26, 27).

Scripture: Deuteronomy 11:26-32
Song: "Sweet Peace, the Gift of God's Love"

At the medical office where I work, I opened the receptionist window to help a patient. "Where's the doctor? I've been waiting for 45 minutes. I need to be somewhere in an hour," she yelled in my face. I was caught off guard as her anger flared.

My heart pounded. I couldn't yell back, or I'd lose my job. *What's the professional response to this?* More importantly, how would God want me to respond? I knew I could reply with love . . . but how would that look? Her side: this lady clearly felt her needs weren't being met. My side: I felt verbally attacked for something over which I had no control.

Romans 12:18 says, "If it is possible, as far as it depends on you, live at peace with everyone." God's command to love one another was so applicable here. I could respond from a heart of love for hurting, broken people or yell back, ramping up the hatred in an already charged situation. How difficult it is sometimes to calm down and make the right choice.

When I've chosen to love, forgive, and try to understand another's feelings, I've always felt better. As it says in Proverbs 14:30, "A heart at peace gives life to the body." What a blessing for simply obeying His Word!

Thank You, **Lord,** for helping me remain calm when others are angry—and for blessing me with peace when I daily choose to obey You. Through Christ, amen.

From Destructive to Divine

See I set before you today life and prosperity, death and destruction. For I command you today to love the LORD your God, to walk in obedience to him (Deuteronomy 30:15, 16).

Scripture: Deuteronomy 30:11-20
Song: "It Is Well with My Soul"

It started with two airliners crashing into two skyscrapers, killing more than 2,600 people. Could anything have been more difficult for our country?

One minute, images of the good life on a clear, blue-sky September 11 morning amid the high-rise buildings of New York City; the next minute, death and destruction as the first airplane hit the World Trade Center, the beginning of an event now known as 9/11. Where were you when you heard the news?

In the aftermath, a two-ton, 20-foot-high, cross-shaped steel beam was found in the wreckage, perhaps a reminder that, no matter what, God hasn't deserted us. Even though this was the worst national tragedy many of us have known in our lifetimes, it provided an opportunity to turn to God. Many did.

For years since this devastating event, volunteers and professionals have worked to restore, rebuild, and protect this city and our country. Communities have created memorials and held fund-raisers, and many have donated to these organizations and continue to pray for the victims' families. Even amidst this great evil, God is working to bring redemption and new life.

O Lord, no matter how great the destruction, nothing is beyond Your repair when I choose to walk in Your ways. When I've created my own life's disasters, because of bad choices, You've rescued and restored me too. In the name of Jesus, amen.

How the Spirit Leads

We are witnesses of these things, and so is the Holy Spirit, whom God has given to those who obey him (Acts 5:32).

Scripture: Acts 5:27-42
Song: "Holy Spirit, Rain Down"

When you've chosen to share the gospel, didn't it seem as if everything just fell into place? My friend, Tammy, taught a church group in Singapore. Before the church meeting, she was reading 1 Corinthians 1:10-13 about divisions in the church. The importance of unity stuck in her mind.

At her meeting, a lady said she quit going to church years ago because of hurtful things that were said to her by other members in the congregation. Tammy shared this Scripture with her, and the woman decided to try church again.

When Tammy's family was deciding to leave Singapore to go back to the United States, she was torn between her ministry and preparing to move. At the most practical level, she dreaded the time-consuming planning for an overseas move. She prayed about it, and when reading John 21:15-17, where Jesus urged Simon Peter to "feed my sheep," she felt as if the Holy Spirit was directing her to keep feeding her own "sheep" in Singapore. The result: The move preparation went effortlessly, giving her time to continue leading her group for several more months.

Similarly, in Acts, the disciples' testimony was directed and confirmed by the Holy Spirit. Thankfully, this same Spirit of God is given to all who respond to Him with obedience.

Father, give me the courage to trust the guidance from the indwelling Holy Spirit in my life's decisions. And let my love for You lead others to You! Through Christ, amen.

Same Temptations Today

The woman said to the serpent, "We may eat fruit from the trees in the garden, but God did say, 'You must not eat fruit from the tree that is in the middle of the garden, and you must not touch it, or you will die'" (Genesis 3:2, 3).

Scripture: Genesis 3:1-7
Song: "Dear Lord, Thou Art the Tree of Life"

Feeding our bodies and souls is about choices and consequences. The Bible says God gave us plants, birds, and some animals to eat—not candy bars, cheese puffs, and soda pop! God wants us to make good choices . . . for our good. When we exercise and make wise food choices, we stay healthy and in shape.

Likewise, when we make choices that feed our souls, we will stay ready to serve God. And He gave us plenty to pick from His garden. The fruits of the Spirit are our food for the soul— "love, joy, peace, patience, kindness, goodness, faithfulness, gentleness and self-control" (see Galatians 5:22, 23).

Moderation in everything applies not only to the food we eat, but to what we feed our souls. If we don't nourish our souls in spending time with God, in reading His Word, and in praying, our love for others could wither and die.

Eve wasn't listening to God when she made her choice in the Garden of Eden. The enemy's subtle way of distorting and deceiving her made eating the forbidden fruit too tempting. Let us beware of the same kind of temptations that come to us on any day of the week.

Lord, thank You for providing so abundantly, giving me so many choices. Give me Your wisdom in my decision-making this day! In Jesus' name, amen.

You Still Have the Lord

By the sweat of your brow you will eat your food until you return to the ground, since from it you were taken; for dust you are and to dust you will return (Genesis 3:19).

Scripture: Genesis 3:18-24
Song: "To God Alone Be the Glory"

We'd already lost thousands of dollars overnight. "Do you think we should take half our 401(k) money, move it to cash, and sell the house?" I asked my husband as we sipped our morning coffee, while the stock market continued to drop several million dollars a second.

Our house was the home in the country I'd always wanted—a Cape-Cod style on three acres, abutting 80 acres with a panoramic view of the Rocky Mountains. Four months after buying it, my husband came home and announced, "There's going to be a downsizing at work tomorrow." He wouldn't be laid off, we decided. But the next morning, we found we were wrong. In the ensuing months, the stress of debt strained our marriage and brought us to the brink of divorce.

We work hard for a living—"by the sweat of your brow"— but it can all be taken away so quickly. And when we leave this earth, our material possessions won't go with us.

If you feel you have lost it all, you have not. You still have what's in your heart: the gift of God's indwelling Spirit to guide you through the toughest times. Thanks be to God!

Father, I know there are consequences for my actions and inactions. Please help me make my decisions guided by Your wisdom—and guide me to continue Your good works while I'm on earth. In Jesus' name I pray. Amen.

Passing the Blame

[God said]: "Have you eaten from the tree that I commanded you not to eat from?" The man said, "The woman you put here with me—she gave me some fruit from the tree, and I ate it" (Genesis 3:11, 12).

Scripture: Genesis 3:8-17
Song: "Come, Sinners, to the Gospel Feast"

I made a huge error at work. In the computer, I entered the eight-digit account number instead of the dollar amount of a customer's payment. I work with a team of six, and the system is set up so no one can tell who entered what. If I didn't say anything, no one would know the mistake was mine. But if I told my boss, I'd be in big trouble—I was close to losing my job from all the other mistakes I'd made lately. Should I take the blame and confess what I did . . . or do nothing?

My actions would affect many people adversely—the person whose account had the error, coworkers, and my supervisor. So I chose to admit my mistake. I took action to correct it, and the consequences for all concerned weren't as bad as they would have been had I kept silent. (And I kept my job.)

God wants all of us to do what's right and be honest. When Adam passed the blame to Eve, God confronted only them. Yet according to the apostle Paul, the whole human race still lives with the consequences of their choices (see Romans 5:12-21).

Lord God of Heaven and earth, You know what's best for me, yet every life experience offers me the opportunity to make good or bad decisions. Thank You for this freedom, but please remind me that no matter how difficult the trouble, following Your way is always the right way. Through the name of Jesus I pray. Amen.

A Window of Hope

Make a roof for it, leaving below the roof an opening one cubit high all around. Put a door in the side of the ark and make lower, middle and upper decks (Genesis 6:16).

Scripture: Genesis 6:11-22
Song: "Bury Thy Sorrow"

I sat on a plane with a young woman who'd graduated from college 15 months earlier. In spite of a 4.0 G.P.A. and great references, she'd been rejected by medical schools because of low medical test scores. Discouraged, she didn't know what to do. I urged her to pursue some other opportunities, reminding her: When God closes a door, He leaves open a window of hope.

Before Noah built the ark, God gave him specific instructions about its design. The length, height, and depth of the ark prevented it from capsizing in stormy seas.

In His construction plan, God provided windows all around, just below the roof. These contributed light, fresh air, and a most important element—hope. Through these openings, Noah and his family would be able to see when the rains stopped, when the sun began to shine, and when the first evidence of land appeared over the horizon.

When rejection and discouragement tumble into my life, it's easy to think things will never improve. That's when I remember Noah's windows and turn back to God with renewed hope.

Lord, when doors keep slamming shut, I get discouraged. Help me to press into Your will and into Your Word in order to keep moving forward. In Jesus' name, amen.

September 16–22. **Jinny Sherman** is a freelance writer who also mentors women. She loves hiking the hills of Southern Oregon with her husband, Rick. They have two adult children.

One Righteous Person

Go into the boat with all your family, for among all the people of the earth, I can see that you alone are righteous (Genesis 7:1, *New Living Translation*).

Scripture: Genesis 7:1-10
Song: "Rise Up, O Men of God"

Harriet Tubman had some things in common with Noah. They both lived lives that honored God. They stood firm against the evils of their day. They listened to Him and followed His leading, even though at times His instructions must have seemed odd. Noah obeyed, in spite of what was probably strong ridicule from his neighbors. (Who builds a huge boat in the desert?)

Harriet Tubman was born into slavery 40 years before the Civil War. From her birthplace in Maryland, she escaped to Pennsylvania, a free state, but soon returned to rescue members of her family. Over the years, she rescued more than 70 slaves, risking her life to transport them along the network of safe houses known as the Underground Railroad. A devout Christian, she depended on God to protect her and those with her. None of the slaves she guided to freedom were caught.

Let us never underestimate the influence of one godly person in a family or community. Noah and Harriet each made tough decisions and acted courageously. Their actions affected their families—and the whole of humanity—in a major way.

Lord, You know the fear that lurks in my heart. Help me draw courage from the lives of Noah and Harriet Tubman. They were everyday people committed to You, and You accomplished great things through them. I give myself to You this day. Please use me as You will. In Jesus' name, amen.

No Rudder

For forty days the floodwaters grew deeper, covering the ground and lifting the boat high above the earth. As the waters rose higher and higher above the ground, the boat floated safely on the surface (Genesis 7:17, 18, *New Living Translation*).

Scripture: Genesis 7:11-24
Song: "All the Way My Savior Leads Me"

The Coho Ferry in Port Angeles, Washington, is a magnificent seagoing vessel. It cruises in from Vancouver, British Columbia, and makes an arc around a long breakwater, then slides into port and sits awhile. Finally, it executes a quarter turn to connect with the dock, so the cars and passengers can exit from the rear. It takes a skilled captain to perform these maneuvers.

Noah wasn't exactly the captain of the ark. He and his family floated in a massive, barge-like boat without an oar, sail, or rudder. He had no way to steer!

Did he sometimes wish he did? (Or was he so thankful he and his family were safe that he didn't care where God took them?) The reality was that he had to completely trust God to guide them.

When life throws tough things at me—a relative with cancer, a lost job opportunity, back or neck pain that keep me awake at night—I can focus on a few marvelous facts: the Sovereign Lord is with me, and He knows where I am. He has plans for me that are for my good, and He will steer a wise course for me.

Gracious Lord, sometimes I get myself into awkward messes, and sometimes life blindsides me. But whatever the situation, You know a way out. When life is uncertain, help me trust that, if I will humble myself, You will guide me. In Christ, amen.

Snapshot of Encouragement

The waters continued to recede until the tenth month, and on the first day of the tenth month the tops of the mountains became visible (Genesis 8:5).

Scripture: Genesis 8:1-12
Song: "Trusting Jesus"

Our son, Joshua, was born 11 weeks early. Though I was excited to see him, fear knotted my muscles. Would he survive?

A few days later, Joshua lay on his side, a rubber glove hovering behind him. Every few seconds it inflated and thumped him on the back. I raised my eyebrows to the nurse.

"Joshua's breathing pattern is typical for premature babies. He takes a breath, waits, and forgets to breathe again, so his heart slows down. He'll grow out of it."

I certainly hoped so! Later, a doctor introduced herself and said, "I have your son's heart problem under control." Heart problem? She left, and my body began trembling. *O God, help!*

Next morning at church, I sidestepped to avoid a blond, blue-eyed youngster who whizzed past. I gasped. Joshua had the same coloring. Instantly, I imagined what he might look like as a healthy boy. That snapshot of encouragement buoyed me until we brought Joshua safely home.

After the rain stopped, Noah and his family remained in the ark for nine months without sight of land. Had God forgotten them? No, just one glimpse of land gave them hope—they would be out of the ark soon.

God of hope, I praise You! When everything around me looks bleak, give me the eyes of faith to wait for Your plan and Your timing. In Jesus' name, amen.

Switching Decades

Then Noah built an altar to the LORD, and there he sacrificed as burnt offerings the animals and birds that had been approved for that purpose (Genesis 8:20, *New Living Translation*).

Scripture: Genesis 8:13-22
Song: "Great Is Thy Faithfulness"

I'm about to switch decades. Birthdays with zeroes after them used to make me groan or sink into the blues, but I've chosen a new attitude. I've discovered that age transitions are easier for me when I have a party with my closest friends. With that to look forward to, I don't focus on my increasing age.

This year my prayer partners and confidantes will gather at a nearby lake for a barbecue picnic. We'll hike, talk, and laugh. But some time during the day, we'll sing "Great Is Thy Faithfulness" to thank God for the many ways He's helped us all during the 20 years we've known each other.

After Noah's long ordeal, he built an altar to worship the Lord, who had protected and provided. Noah built the ark out of *obedience*, but he created the altar out of *devotion*.

Each year, I recount in a journal what God has done and thank Him for the many answers to prayer, miracles for family and friends, and other blessings. From these recollections, I gain wisdom and courage to face today's challenges—and the faith to trust Him for tomorrow.

Great God, thank You for life, for friends and loved ones, and for years to enjoy them. Give me eyes to see all You do and a humble heart to praise You for Your mercies, which are new every morning. In Jesus' name, amen.

The Fruit of Blessing

God blessed Noah and his sons, saying to them, "Be fruit-ful and increase in number and fill the earth" (Genesis 9:1).

Scripture: Genesis 9:1-7
Song: "The Lord Bless Thee"

"The Lord bless you and keep you . . . and give you peace" (Numbers 6:24, 26). My husband and I gave that blessing to Josh and Anna every evening. We never knew when we started this tradition with our children what a vast influence it would have on them.

When Josh and Anna were teens, a woman approached me after Vacation Bible School and said, "This week there were two young people who worked hard, had good attitudes, and were always dependable."

"How nice," I said.

"Since they don't look alike, I didn't realize they were related."
Why is she telling me this?

"Josh and Anna were great all week," the woman explained.

I blinked. My kids? Pictures of untidy rooms, bickering, and resistance to chores flashed through my mind. "Really?" I had no idea they were so cooperative with *other* adults!

"They were a great blessing."

"Thank you." I wanted to take the credit for raising such great kids. The character traits she mentioned were beyond what I had taught them. This fruit came from God's work in their lives.

Lord, Your blessing on Noah and his children enabled them to fulfill their task on earth. Thank You that You bless Your children. And thank You that when You assign me a task, You give me what I need to fulfill it. Through Christ I pray. Amen.

A Colorful Crescent

Whenever . . . the rainbow appears in the clouds, I will remember my covenant between me and you and all living creatures of every kind. Never again will the waters become a flood to destroy all life (Genesis 9:14, 15).

Scripture: Genesis 9:8-17
Song: "Blessed Be Your Name"

The first rainbow's brilliant hues arched over Noah's family to remind them of God's covenant and to bring them joy after their long ordeal. When I was 8-years-old, my dad was in a head-on freeway collision. Doctors told him he would never walk again. Sadness consumed me. Daddy, who loved to hike, bike, and swim—on crutches for the rest of his life?

I had no way of knowing then the important lessons I would learn because of this calamity. The first I learned by watching Dad's determination. He exercised his leg several times a day and eventually proved the doctors wrong. After physical therapy and several surgeries, he learned not only to walk but to run.

Second, I observed genuine love, as my parents stuck together to work for Dad's recovery. True friendship was illustrated as people from church brought delicious meals every evening.

Dad's accident turned our household upside down for six months. But the examples I witnessed—of perseverance, commitment, and friendship—have arched over my life like a rainbow, adding wisdom and beauty. They have also shaped my adult responses to tough situations.

Lord, when I'm in the thick of a frightening situation, I tend to shrink with fear. But You are able to do far more than I can imagine. Remind me! In the name of Jesus, amen.

Be a Man

Brace yourself like a man; I will question you, and you shall answer me (Job 38:3).

Scripture: Job 38:1-7
Song: "God of Wonders"

Life as the mother of three teenage boys can be baffling. Seth, the oldest, picked on the youngest, Sam. Sam retaliated. Seth blocked his swing and, in the process, inadvertently gave Sam a bloody nose. Sam ran to the bathroom, dealt with the blood, and returned to his brother. "I'm sorry," he said.

"You're the one with the bloody nose, Bud." Seth's voice was full of apology. Sam's reply? "I'd rather get a broken nose by you than anyone else." Male bonding makes no sense to me.

I felt the same when I read God's words to Job. Throughout the Bible we have many men whining to God, questioning Him. The psalmist, for example, tells us to pour our complaints out before God. Yet here's Job, who has suffered beyond comprehension, and God tells him to . . . *be a man.*

I would have brewed Job a cup of tea and pulled out the tissue box. But God told Job to buck up—and then systemically reminded him of how small he was compared to God's majesty. Later in Job 42:5, Job tells the Lord, "My ears had heard of you but now my eyes see you." That kind of bonding makes all the sense in the world!

Holy God, sometimes when I complain I'm forgetting who You are. Forgive my arrogance and receive my praise, through Christ my Lord. Amen.

September 23–29. **Paula Moldenhauer** longs to be close enough to God to breathe His fragrance. A freelance writer and mom of four, she and her husband live in Colorado.

Deep Places

Have you journeyed to the springs of the sea or walked in the recesses of the deep? . . . Have you comprehended the vast expanses of the earth? Tell me, if you know all this (Job 38:16, 18).

Scripture: Job 38:12-18
Song: "O the Deep, Deep Love of Jesus"

The tour guide leads through the recesses of a cave, commenting on the stalactites, then turns out the lights. The dark penetrates. Climbing a *fourteener* mountain is the opposite kind of experience. I break tree-line and push to the peak. There is nothing but light and sky above, expansive vistas below. And if I stand at ocean edge, I'm reminded some things are too vast—too deep and too wide—to comprehend. Each encounter leaves me breathless.

Then I think of God, and how creation proclaims His character. The view from the peak or at the edge of the ocean is farther than I can see, yet Scripture says my sins are removed from me as far is the east is from the west. God is more majestic than the mountains. He is the light that penetrates any darkness. His love is deeper than the ocean.

Preachers tell me to dive into the ocean of God. I want to. But the temptation is just to splash around in a little pond of intermittent devotion. Yet there is nothing to fear. As the old song says, "The deep, deep love of Jesus . . . rolling as a mighty ocean in its fullness over me."

Lord, no matter how deeply I dive or how far I walk, I can't grasp the measureless wonders of this earth—or the magnificence of Your love. Through Christ, amen.

Great God, Great Care

Do you send the lightning bolts on their way? Do they report to you, "Here we are"? (Job 38:35).

Scripture: Job 38:28-38
Song: "Indescribable"

Growing up in the foothills of the Ozarks, I understand the term gully-washer, am well-acquainted with razor-sharp jags of lightning, and have been startled awake by thunder rumbling like the throaty voice of a great giant. My children have less experience with such things. It storms in Colorado, but our home, sheltered by the Rockies, hasn't seen too many gully-washers. Yet this summer the heavens opened and unleashed floods of raging rivers down our neighborhood streets. Awed, the kids watched out the windows in fascination.

One thing my children have known is the wonder of snow. What delight to watch them as little ones, twirling in the softly falling white, mouths wide open—or standing stock still, eyes full of amazement as they studied a single, perfect, starlike flake captured on a finger.

Camping in the mountains, we see the white stars glisten like diamonds on black velvet, more than we can count. We're well aware of how small we are and how little we know. Yet it's a good thing to be "put in our place" as we marvel at God's creation, isn't it? Good to know that such a great God cares so greatly for you and for me.

Amazing Lord, only You understand all the intricacies of Your creation. Only You put the stars in place, send the lightning bolts, and make the snowflake. You are unfathomable, and so my heart swells with worship, in the name of Jesus. Amen.

Saved by His Mighty Arm

Do you have an arm like God's, and can your voice thunder like his? (Job 40:9).

Scripture: Job 40:6-14
Song: "Sheltered in the Arms of God"

What started out as a playful outing to watch a sea turtle turned into a brutal buffeting of waves. My husband and I swam around a jutting point of rock, hoping to enter the calmer Hawaiian bay on the other side of it. I fought not only the great Pacific Ocean, but the rising panic within. *Father, help me not be so afraid.*

Calm came over me. Then I was submerged, somersaulting, and pulled out to sea. Miraculously, I didn't fight. Completely relaxed, I was an underwater rag doll.

Suddenly I felt myself rising. As my head broke the surface I gasped for air and looked into the white face of my husband. He'd watched me being taken from him and, in a valiant effort, anchored himself by wrapping one strong arm around a coral reef while reaching for me with the other. He grabbed my swimsuit and, leveraging himself on the coral, pulled with all his might. His arm was a bloody mess . . . but I lived.

Jerry's strong arm (strengthened by God's) saved me. Though a good swimmer, I had been totally incapable of helping myself. If I'd tried, I would have fought against the arm reaching for me. Trapped in the undertow, I would have perished.

Mighty God, sometimes I think too much of myself, flexing puny muscles in Your face. Fighting too-big battles, I strive on my own, rejecting Your sovereign will. Forgive me. You are the only one adorned in glory. Praise to You, through Jesus. Amen.

What to Do?

The LORD must be furious . . . because our ancestors did not obey the laws written in this book. Go find out what the LORD wants us to do (2 Chronicles 34:21, *Contemporary English Version*).

Scripture: 2 Chronicles 34:14-21
Song: "Song of Confession"

The younger boys and I memorized Scripture about the attributes of God—one for each letter of the alphabet. The passage of the day focused on *M* for God's *mercy* and was found in Daniel 9:9, 10.

"The Lord our God is merciful and forgiving, even though we have rebelled against him; we have not obeyed the Lord our God or kept the laws he gave us." I don't remember what the altercation of the morning was. Sibling squabbles ended in unkind words and hurt feelings—and Mom's impatient response. A tired, home-schooling Momma, I cried out to God and asked what we should do to survive the morning's struggles.

We had a family powwow and, before long, had talked through the problems, forgiving each other. Then we prayed for God's forgiveness and empowerment to do better.

All of a sudden my youngest looked at me with eyes lit with understanding. "It's like that verse, Mom. We sinned against God by the way we acted—but He is merciful and forgives us!"

Heavenly Father, thanks to Your Son's cross, I know what to do when I sin—come to You for forgiveness and the power to change. Thank You for Your mercy, even when I rebel against You. Please change me from the inside out so I can be more like Jesus. In His name I pray. Amen.

He Keeps Forgiving

Because your heart was responsive and you humbled yourself before God . . . because you humbled yourself before me and tore your robes and wept in my presence, I have heard you, declares the LORD (2 Chronicles 34:27).

Scripture: 2 Chronicles 34:22-28
Song: "Redeemed, Restored, Forgiven"

I've never torn my robes over my sins, but the good Lord has seen plenty of weeping in His presence. I thought I was humble. I was certainly unhappy with myself, aware of my shortcomings, and imploring Him to change me.

A spiritual perfectionist, I kept trying to do better. I didn't understand that heaping condemnation upon myself didn't make me humble; instead, punishing myself spurned God's grace.

Thankfully, God heard my cries. Humbling came in the form of four children in six years. Here's what I mean: My deepest desire was to be a good mother, so I determined that I'd *always* be fun and cheerful and *never* lose my temper.

But I soon realized I couldn't be the perfect mom, and I found it impossible to let myself off the hook. As I groveled before the Lord, repenting once again, He whispered to my heart, *Do you really think I didn't know you would sin today? That it surprised me? My grace is for every sin you've committed . . . and every sin you will commit.*

As I accepted grace, He changed me. I became more humble before Him, not less, as I stopped living in condemnation.

Father, sometimes in my efforts to please You, I forget how much I need You. Teach me the kind of humility that relies on my need of Your grace. In Jesus' name, amen.

Still Full of Ourselves?

Come, let us build ourselves a city, with a tower that reaches to the heavens, so that we may make a name for ourselves (Genesis 11:4).

Scripture: Genesis 11:1-9
Song: "Clothe Yourself with Humility"

The 100th anniversary of the launching—and sinking—of the Titanic was April 2012. Perhaps the most famous quote about that mighty vessel is, "God himself cannot sink this ship." While this pronouncement was likely a product of Hollywood, not history, it is accurate to say that—before it sailed—the Titanic was indeed considered beyond any potential harm. When the New York office of White Star Lines heard that the ship was possibly in trouble, a vice president announced: "We place absolute confidence in the Titanic. We believe the boat is unsinkable."

It wasn't just the shipbuilders who bought into the idea. Before boarding the Titanic, one passenger wrote home, "We are changing ships and coming home in a new unsinkable boat."

Ouch. I guess we humans never learn. Thousands of years before the Titanic sailed, we were already bragging on our great accomplishments. The builders of the Tower of Babel lauded their newfound ability to make better bricks, saying their tower would reach the heavens, and they would be famous. We are still full of ourselves, even after 6,000 years.

Father, I have the audacity to think I'm incapable of the arrogance of the builders of the Titanic or the tower of Babel. Then I'm shocked when something I've built my hope upon fails. There is nothing worthy of my complete faith except You. Help me build on the Rock alone! In Jesus' name I pray. Amen.

Recalculating!

By faith Abraham . . . obeyed . . . went out, not know-ing where he was going (Hebrews 11:8, *New American Standard Bible*).

Scripture: Hebrews 11:8-16
Song: "Lead On, O King Eternal"

On my first trip in my new 30-foot RV, I found myself in road construction on I-90, along the northern border of Indiana. Traffic was bumper-to-bumper but flowing at 75 mph. I was sandwiched between semis, so close I could see my reflection in the rearview mirror of the one in front of me. Suddenly my lane became an exit, and I was totally lost.

A few years later I bought a GPS, which keeps that from happening again. As long as it knows my destination, it talks me through all confusion, patiently suggesting, "Make a legal U-turn when possible" when I miss a turn, and offering, "Recalculating" when I've gone hopelessly astray.

I see my GPS as a symbol of the Holy Spirit. He too knows exactly where I'm supposed to be going and the best way for me to travel. He doesn't lose patience when I willfully go off in my own direction, but reminds me to turn around, go back, and regain my focus. I can almost hear Him whispering, "Recalculating!"

Loving Father, thank You for guiding me! Thank You for continuing to love me, even when I wander off after my own ideas and desires, even when I foolishly turn my back on You. Help me to trust You and follow You, through Christ my Lord. Amen.

September 30. **Elsi Dodge,** of Boulder, Colorado, sings, coleads Bible study, works with a youth group, and travels in an RV when she's not writing.

My Prayer Notes
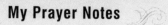

DEVOTIONS®

OCTOBER

Your kingdom is an everlasting kingdom . . . The LORD is trustworthy in all he promises and faithful in all he does.

—Psalm 145:13

Gary Wilde, Editor   **Margaret Williams,** Project Editor   Photo © iStockphoto | Thinkstock®

DEVOTIONS® is published quarterly by Standard Publishing, Cincinnati, Ohio, www.standardpub.com. © 2012 by Standard Publishing. All rights reserved. Topics based on the Home Daily Bible Readings, International Sunday School Lessons. © 2010 by the Committee on the Uniform Series. Printed in the U.S.A. All Scripture quotations, unless otherwise indicated, are taken from the *HOLY BIBLE, NEW INTERNATIONAL VERSION®. NIV®.* Copyright © 2011 by Biblica, Inc.™ Used by permission of Zondervan. All rights reserved. The *New American Standard Bible®* (*NASB*). Copyright © 1960, 1962, 1963, 1968, 1971, 1972, 1973, 1975, 1977, 1995 by The Lockman Foundation. Used by permission. (www.Lockman.org). All rights reserved. The Holy Bible, *New Living Translation* (*NLT*). Copyright © 1996, 2004. Used by permission of Tyndale House Publishers, Inc., Wheaton, Illinois 60189. All rights reserved. *The Living Bible* (*TLB*) copyright © 1971. Used by permission of Tyndale House Publishers, Inc., Carol Stream, Illinois 60188. All rights reserved.

When the Checkbook Follows

Abram took Sarai his wife and Lot his nephew, and all their possessions which they had accumulated, and the persons which they had acquired in Haran, and they set out for the land of Canaan (Genesis 12:5, *New American Standard Bible*).

Scripture: Genesis 12:1-7
Song: "I Surrender All"

I've been on the road in my RV for eight weeks at a time, perfectly content with a week's worth of clothes. I carry my printer and computer with me, my bedding, dog and cat food—really, the only things I miss from my house are books. (However, e-book readers keep me from feeling too deprived in that area.)

I think about my house and all that it contains. I've accumulated so much stuff: what would Abram think? Yes, at home I need clothes for church and for winter, and I have hundreds of books that I treasure. But do I really need all this?

I walk through a superstore humming "I Surrender All," picking up a pretty shirt, an attractive knickknack, and a gift for a friend next Christmas, not considering whether these purchases are essential.

My financial advisor glares at me when I impulsively give money to a missionary, orphanage, or homeless shelter. But those are probably my best moments—when my heart and God's are aligned . . . and my checkbook follows.

O God, thank You for loving me so much, for being so bountiful and generous to me. Give me Your heart, and loosen my grip on my possessions. Through Christ, amen.

October 1–6. **Elsi Dodge**, of Boulder, Colorado, sings, coleads Bible study, works with a youth group, and travels in an RV when she's not writing.

Gift of Gratitude

Go, walk through the length and breadth of the land, for I am giving it to you (Genesis 13:17).

Scripture: Genesis 13:8-18
Song: "All Creatures of Our God and King"

My family was really good at giving and receiving gifts. No ripping open the wrapping paper, calling out "thanks!" and moving on—not for us. First, you admired the paper, read the card aloud, and tried to guess what was inside, while those in the know chuckled and hinted. Then you opened your present. You removed it from its packaging and held it up, looking at it closely, admiring and commenting on details.

"Oh, thank you! I love this author, and the title is fascinating. Look at the beautiful illustrations . . . and it has that wonderful new-book smell too. Thank you so much!" We could take five hours opening Christmas presents—and there were only three of us.

How dare I give the Lord less gratitude than I do my friends at Christmas? Abram walked every inch of the land God gave him, seeing the details, thanking the Lord for His gift.

But how do I pray? My tendency is to rush straight to requests: "Please heal John, and help Sue find another job, and give Annette a safe trip." When I do remember to slow down and start by thanking the Lord, I find my own soul is blessed—a precious gift!

O Father, thank You for this day! I loved seeing the sunrise reflecting off the mountain peaks this morning, the snow and clouds melting together in pink and gold. Thank You for all the blessings You pour into my life each day. In Jesus' name, amen.

Every Breath I Take

No longer shall your name be called Abram, but your name shall be Abraham; for I have made you the father of a multitude of nations (Genesis 17:5, *New American Standard Bible*).

Scripture: Genesis 17:1-8
Song: "Breathe on Me, Breath of Life"

The boy shifted uncomfortably in his chair at the conference table as his parents, the social worker, and I discussed the details of his transfer to my classroom.

"You know," I said to him, "your file here says you're David. Your teacher has been calling you Dave, and your mom calls you Davie. What do you want me to call you?"

He sat a moment, apparently thinking. "Maybe Christopher?" he suggested, then looked baffled when we laughed.

Maybe you were named for a grandparent, or you changed your name to erase a painful connection. (And did I mention there's no E on the end of my name, Elsi?) Names are important because they seem to define us, reflect who we are.

The Lord changed people's names throughout the Bible, often giving a new name to highlight a new responsibility or gift. But when He changed Abram ("exalted father") to Abraham ("father of many") and Sarai ("my princess") to Sarah ("princess"), He did more than that. He added an aspirant—the breathy H-sound—to each name. In a sense, He breathed into them a fresh breath of life (see Genesis 2:7 and John 20:22).

You've given me new life, **Lord**, and I'm so grateful. Everything changed when You came into my heart. Help me take in Your love and forgiveness with every breath and share those incomparable gifts each time I exhale. In Jesus' name, amen.

Promise? Really?

I took your father Abraham from the land beyond the Euphrates and led him throughout Canaan and gave him many descendants. I gave him Isaac (Joshua 24:3).

Scripture: Joshua 24:1-13
Song: "God Said It, I Believe It"

"Are we going to lunch, Grandma?" My friend smiled at her little granddaughter. "Yes, dear, as soon as I'm done here."

"OK!" The child ran off. Soon another grandchild appeared. "Are we really going to lunch, Grandma? Are you sure? Are we really?"

"Really," my friend said firmly.

"But Grandma, do you promise?"

"Honey, I told you we are. And I've never lied to you, have I? You can count on it!"

It was interesting to compare the two children. One believed her grandmother and was willing to play patiently until it was time to leave. The other couldn't stop worrying that what her grandmother had said wouldn't really happen. The grandmother hadn't ever lied to either child, but one was able to trust; the other was fearful.

Which am I? I wondered as we waited. Do I trust the Lord, or do I nag Him, asking if He really means what He said?

That's what the Lord was saying to the Israelites: "Hey, you can trust me! I've always done what I told you I'd do, haven't I? So you can believe me this time too."

Loving Father, You've given me no reason to doubt, but I still wonder sometimes. Help me believe Your Word. In Christ I pray. Amen.

Make Time for the Lord

Look to the LORD and his strength; seek his face always. Remember the wonders he has done (Psalm 105:4, 5).

Scripture: Psalm 105:1-11
Song: "What a Friend We Have in Jesus"

King Soopers, my Boulder, Colorado, grocery store, has recently installed a computerized system to keep track of the number of customers and available checkout lanes. This keeps the lines short and makes the customers happy.

There's one problem, though. When the manager says, "We're opening another lane and can take you right over here, ma'am," I refuse.

"Thanks, but I'm happy to wait for Dave King," I say. And the manager sighs and asks someone else. Often there are six or eight of us in Dave's line, while other checkers stand idle. I call us the "Dave King fan club."

Waiting patiently in line, I remember Dave's smiling face. He knows our names, makes eye contact with each of his customers, and makes us feel we're the most important person in the store. I'm more than willing to stand in line to have a few moments with him. It seems to make the whole day go better.

What are some of the wonders the Lord has done for me? Well, there's sunshine, the smell of spring, soft beagle ears, good books, friends, the Bible, salvation . . . I could go on and on. Today may I eagerly make time to seek His face, talk with Him, feel His love, and read His Word.

Lord, thanks for smiling at me, listening to me, and speaking to me through Your Word. When I wait for You, the whole day goes better! In Jesus' name, amen.

Star-Namer

"Now look toward the heavens, and count the stars, if you are able to count them." And He said to him, "So shall your descendants be" (Genesis 15:5, *New American Standard Bible*).

Scripture: Genesis 15:5-21
Song: "Trust in the Promise"

"It's one o'clock in the morning! You said we could go see the Perseid meteor shower."

The Boulder Church must have the only teens in the nation whose youth group is led by two women who are over 60 years old. At this August retreat, Vicki and I were in a mountain house with 11 girls, 5th grade through college age.

We sat on blankets, eyes fixed on the sky. Nothing happened. Finally, someone said, "Let's sing!" Lying on the deck, staring at the stars, we sang. And—I'm not making this up—as we got to the line, "You placed the stars in the sky and You call them by name," we saw a shooting star. Then another, and another.

Someone started "Amazing Grace," and the meteors came again. "I think they're coming because we're singing," a girl said in awed tones. We sang for an hour or so, until sleepiness and the chilly night air drove us back inside.

I was humming as I crawled back into my bed. He made the stars, uncountable, and spread them throughout the heavens. The stars sang at creation, and the Bible confidently says God knows each one by name. He knows your name too.

Abba Father, You know my name, and my heart, my fears and worries, my sins, my desire to be with You. I am loved by the Creator of the universe. Amazing! All praise and glory to You, in the name of Your Son, Jesus. Amen.

He's There, in Joy and Sadness

Haran died in the presence of his father Terah in the land of his birth, in Ur of the Chaldeans (Genesis 11:28, *New American Standard Bible*).

Scripture: Genesis 11:27-32
Song: "Now Thank We All Our God"

"My lilacs are finally blooming, and the bush is so full this year," I told my husband. I felt excited as I admired the lavender blooms. But my mood was marred by sorrow, as I glanced at the empty house just beyond my backyard fence, recalling Alice's recent death. *Who will I give my lilacs to this year?*

Alice loved lilacs and their scent but didn't have any bushes, so I shared mine with her for more than two decades. She'd wanted to die in the home she'd shared with her husband for 40 years, so my sadness grew deeper as I thought of how she died in a hospital among strangers. *I've got to shake this sorrowful attitude, or the rest of the day will be gloomy.*

But then I recalled a tree-lined highway from a recent road trip. What caught my attention were the intermittent dark green pines peeking out among the other varieties of bright green trees. The scene called to mind the occasional dark spots that creep in among the bright spots in my life. They are so subtly blended in—and God's presence and blessing are a part of the mix too—a tapestry of joy and sadness.

My dear Lord, You are with me always, in joy and sorrow. I thank You for Your goodness and loving care in every moment of my days. In Jesus' name, amen.

October 7–13. **Bernita Caesar** lives in Arvada, Colorado, with her husband. She enjoys quilting, scrapbooking, and spending time with her children and grandchildren.

Just Ask

Please say that you are my sister so that it may go well with me because of you, and that I may live on account of you (Genesis 12:13, *New American Standard Bible*).

Scripture: Genesis 12:10-20
Song: "Greater Is He That Is in Me"

As I spilled out the story to a trusted friend, I could see the faintly disguised shock on her face. I hadn't told anyone because I was ashamed of my selfishness.

As an eager new Christian, I wore a small gold angel pin on my collar. I asked the Lord to send my way those whom He wanted me to comfort or just listen to. Coworkers often approached me during my break time and began their conversations with comments about my pin. Eventually, I grew weary of these interruptions. Selfishly, I asked God to stop sending me people.

Guess what? He did. After weeks of peaceful, uninterrupted breaks, I noticed the change. *Whoa, I'd better be more careful, because God takes me at my word.*

I wondered what was happening to those who needed some encouragement or a listening ear. I even visualized the disappointment on God's face. It was a wretched time for me.

After I told my friend all of this, she said, "Just apologize and ask God to change things back." Could it be that easy?

Lord, just as Abraham did, I sometimes ask for the wrong things. I can't thank You enough, though, for allowing me to look at myself and giving me a second chance. Please help me not to become weary in Your service, but to keep trusting You for the strength to minister in Your name. Through Jesus Christ I pray. Amen.

Tracking with Sarai

Sarai said to Abram, "Now behold, the LORD has prevented me from bearing children. Please go in to my maid; perhaps I shall obtain children through her." And Abram listened to the voice of Sarai (Genesis 16:2, *New American Standard Bible*).

Scripture: Genesis 16:1-6
Song: "The Christ of Every Crisis"

The speaker placed a large purse on the podium. She removed the contents, one by one, as she continued to speak about the various ways we could pray. For the next 20 minutes, we heard suggestions for time of day and places to use for prayer. She encouraged us to be unique and creative with our choices and not to copy someone else.

Our lecturer also suggested that the format for our daily prayers could start with praise, followed by confession, continuing with intercession, and closing with our petitions.

"When you ask God for help," she continued, "how many of you really leave your answers up to Him?" Then she took the items from the podium and placed them, individually, back into the purse. "Many of us give God our prayers and worries in the morning," she said. "And then, throughout the day, we take them back, one at a time." My eyes were moist as I thought of how I did this too. It was as if I didn't trust God to do things His way without my help. *Sarai, sometimes we're on the same wavelength, aren't we?*

O Lord God, I am sorry for getting in the way of Your work and trying to engineer the circumstances of my life. Please help me to let go and focus more on trusting in Your omnipotent power. In the Holy name of Jesus, amen.

Repairing the Damage

As for Ishmael, I have heard you; behold, I will bless him, and will make him fruitful and will multiply him exceedingly. He shall become the father of twelve princes, and I will make him a great nation (Genesis 17:20, *New American Standard Bible*).

Scripture: Genesis 17:18-22
Song: "Jesus Is the Answer"

"Now what should I do?" I moaned. I'd discovered a large hole at the bottom edge of the beautiful new friendship shawl I was knitting. It was well over halfway completed, and somewhere along the way I had dropped stitches. The thought of ripping out many inches of work was daunting, so I decided to try and repair it.

The task reminded me of Ishmael's situation. Though he was Abraham's son, he wasn't eligible for the covenant. Abraham knew he and Sarah had made a mistake, and he was concerned for Ishmael's future. God told Abraham He had a plan and would take care of Ishmael, thus repairing the damage, promising to make Ishmael's descendants into a strong, great nation.

I needed a plan too. Before starting, I said a quick prayer because the work would be slow and tedious. Yet the result turned out to be worth my time and effort. Not only did I reinforce the base of the shawl, but the new work blended in perfectly with the whole pattern (just as God does with His plans for us).

O my God, I so often jump ahead of Your plans and make serious mistakes. Please help me to stop, listen, and rely on Your wisdom as You strengthen my life's foundation. I pray this in the name of Jesus. Amen.

Why Pray When You Can Worry?

The matter distressed Abraham greatly because of his son
(Genesis 21:11, *New American Standard Bible*).

Scripture: Genesis 21:8-14
Song: "I'll Walk with God"

The sign on a neighborhood church said, "Why Pray When You Can Worry?" This seemed like a strange saying to me as a child, and I used to laugh at it.

Now I'm doing it! In fact I'm known as "the family worrier," and my children joke about it, but I'm not amused. The older I get the more frequently it happens. Even after I think I've left my dismal projections of the future with God, I spend the rest of the day wondering how He's going to help me. My tendency to worry makes me feel as if I'm letting God down.

I've noticed that Abraham usually brought his worries to God, or so it seems, and mostly he waited for God's timing. When he didn't, though, God responded with forgiveness and mercy.

I haven't found a solution to my worrying, but my current plan is to walk more closely with God by talking to Him about every care, large or small. I know this will make my concerns lighter on my shoulders.

There is a tiny wooden sign in my kitchen that says, "Trust in the Lord with all your heart" (Proverbs 3:5). I'll try to take notice of that little plaque more often while reminding myself of the New Testament version: "Cast all your anxiety on him because he cares for you" (1 Peter 5:7).

Faithful God, I know that when I worry, I lose strength for the day. Please give me the grace to keep looking up amidst all circumstances. In Jesus' precious name, amen.

Tie a Knot and Hang On

Sarah died in Kireath-arba (that is, Hebron) in the land of Canaan; and Abraham went in to mourn for Sarah and to weep for her (Genesis 23:2, *New American Standard Bible*).

Scripture: Genesis 23:1-6
Song: "Through It All"

Not again, Lord; it's too much too soon. I had just learned that a friend lost her husband unexpectedly. They were on vacation when he collapsed in a motel room, dying the next day at the hospital. She was the fourth friend of mine who'd lost her husband in the past six months. They'd become widows with no warning.

I'm not sure whether my anguish was from grief or fear that it could happen to me. *I know that You give us trials to make us strong, Lord, but this seems like too much.* I wondered how I would cope with such a heavy, seemingly impossible burden, the kind my friends were facing.

I'm not sure why, but the phrase "tie a knot and hang on" came to mind. It seemed to be God's answer to my earlier prayer. I remembered a large rope I'd seen hanging from a barn with thick knots up the length of it. I saw the rope as God's support, with each knot as either a snag or a handhold.

Abraham has been a good example for me. He mourned Sarah and buried her. Then he trusted the Lord for his next move, just as he'd done all along his journey.

Almighty and faithful Lord, help me to cling to You in times of need. Remind me to trust in Your support and hang on to Your promises. In the name of the Father, the Son, and the Holy Spirit, I pray. Amen.

A Laughing Matter

Is anything too difficult for the LORD? At the appointed time I will return to you, at this time next year, and Sarah will have a son (Genesis 18:14, *New American Standard Bible*).

Scripture: Genesis 17:15-17; 18:9-15; 21:1-7
Song: "God Will Take Care of You"

"This is a surprise! Where are you moving?" said yet another neighbor. She had just seen the unexpected "For Sale" sign in our yard. To each of the inquiries regarding location, schools, and my husband's job (which was ending soon), I had to answer: "We don't know yet."

This was the biggest step my husband and I had ever taken. We were fairly new at leaving decisions in God's hands, so it was a weird and funny situation, although scary. I wasn't sure how to explain it.

I thought of Sarah conceiving Isaac in her 90s. Isaac's name means "laughter," and both Sarah and Abraham did laugh when they heard God foretell the birth of the child. Their son became a permanent reminder, both for them and all generations, that God can be trusted, even when the situation seems laughable.

Well, we sold our home in three weeks, months sooner than expected. Then our out-of-state buyer allowed us to rent it back until the end of the school year. My husband had a job interview two hours after we closed on our new home, and he was hired. God worked out the details in His own way—and better than we could have imagined.

Dear Lord, thank You for Your wise guidance in my life. Please increase my faith and help me to trust in Your timing, no matter how unexplainable. In Jesus' name, amen.

Righteous Faith

Abram believed the LORD, and he credited it to him as righteousness (Genesis 15:6).

Scripture: Genesis 15:1-6
Song: "Faith Is the Victory"

"Ah, here is our very own Abraham," said our minister as he greeted my husband on the first Sunday in our new ministry. He hadn't come across too many men who would leave a lucrative, fulfilling career in the secular world to go into full-time Christian work for a third of the salary.

But it wasn't the first time I'd observed my husband's seemingly casual but committed faith in God. We'd been married only a few months when Roger informed me we'd be moving back to his hometown with seemingly no prospect of jobs. When I asked why, he just said, "I don't know, exactly. But I can't get away from the fact that God has told me we need to go."

So, feeling a little like Abram's wife, Sarai, I packed our few household goods and followed my husband from Texas to Illinois. There I saw firsthand how God confirmed Roger's decision over and over. Now, 17 years later, he unquestioningly followed God to Colorado.

Hudson Taylor once said, "We do not need a great faith, but faith in a great God." Like Abraham and many others before him, Roger believes that what God promises, He accomplishes.

Father, I confess that many times my faith is weak. In my humanness I forget how great You are. I believe—but help my unbelief. In Jesus' name, amen.

October 14–20. **Marjorie Vawter** lives in Colorado and is a freelance editor and writer for various Christian publishers. She has published numerous devotionals.

The God Who Sees

[Hagar] said, "I have now seen the One who sees me" (Genesis 16:13).

Scripture: Genesis 16:7-16
Song: "Open Mine Eyes"

Known as one of the most prolific hymn writers in history, Fanny Crosby penned many of the hymns we still sing today. As a result of an incompetent doctor, Fanny was permanently blinded when she was only 6-weeks-old.

Even though she was physically blind, Fanny wouldn't have it any other way. She said, "It seemed intended by the blessed providence of God that I should be blind all my life, and I thank him for the dispensation. If perfect earthly sight were offered me tomorrow, I would not accept it. I might not have sung hymns to the praise of God if I had been distracted by the beautiful and interesting things about me."

Fanny often spoke of her "spiritual sight" in her hymns. In "Blessed Assurance," for example, she wrote: "visions of rapture now burst on my sight."

As Hagar did, Fanny saw the "well of Thy full salvation that sparkles and flows for me." And she looked forward to the blessed day when she would "see Him face to face" and "know Him by the print of the nails in His hand." As Hagar saw the one who saw her in her need, so also did Fanny Crosby.

Almighty and everlasting God, open my eyes that I may see You, that I may see others as You see them, and that I may see Jesus my Savior and Redeemer. In the name of this same Jesus, who lives and reigns with You and the Holy Spirit, one God, now and forever, amen.

The Ultimate Promise-keeper

You must keep my covenant, you and your descendants after you for the generations to come (Genesis 17:9).

Scripture: Genesis 17:9-14
Song: "Standing on the Promises"

Several weeks ago, our son got married. As the bride and groom exchanged vows, I rejoiced at seeing them willingly enter into their marriage covenant. They chose the traditional vows from the *Book of Common Prayer*: "In the Name of God, I take you to be my wife/husband, to have and to hold from this day forward, for better for worse, for richer for poorer, in sickness and in health, to love and to cherish, until we are parted by death. This is my solemn vow."

Genesis tells us of the vows that were exchanged when God made a covenant with Abraham. Entering into a covenant in Abraham's time was serious business, not taken lightly. God made some pretty awesome promises to Abraham, promises that still stand today. All He asked in return was obedience.

As Randy and Nikki accepted each other's vows, they then exchanged rings as a token of those vows. So God requested a token from Abraham and his descendants when they accepted God's promises—their complete obedience symbolized by circumcision. Similarly, God enters into a covenant relationship with us when we believe and accept the gift of salvation through His Son, Jesus Christ. The symbol? Baptism.

Father, today I recommit my heart, my soul, my life to You. I can do no less when I consider the extent of Your love as You sacrificed Your Son to pay my sin debt. Thank You for Your saving covenant with all who trust in You. In Jesus' name, amen.

God Will Provide

Isaac said, "But where is the lamb for the burnt offering?" Abraham answered, "God himself will provide the lamb for the burnt offering, my son" (Genesis 22:7, 8).

Scripture: Genesis 22:1-8
Song: "Behold! Behold the Lamb of God"

When my husband called me in the middle of the day right after the first of the year, I had no idea how his words would change our lives: "I talked to my boss a little while ago . . . and they're letting me go."

Our country's leaders kept saying we had "turned the corner" and the economy was improving. But the company my husband had worked for during the last 11 years wasn't getting new projects. And they could not afford to keep him on staff.

My first thought was, "What are we going to do?" My income as a freelance editor and writer was sporadic but adequate—as a *supplemental* income. I was already doing as much as I could possibly handle alone. Yet the apostle Paul's words to the Philippians sprang into mind: "My God will meet all your needs according to the riches of his glory in Christ Jesus" (4:19). These words soon became my watchwords of faith.

The job search has lasted nine months now. While we are still waiting on God to provide the job He has for Roger, we have seen His provision, over and over again. Through a variety of people and ways, He has proved faithful.

Father God, You indeed are faithful. You not only provide for my daily needs, You have provided the way of salvation through Your Son, Jesus. I praise You for giving me what I don't deserve and supplying all my needs as well. In Jesus' name, amen.

Faith in Action

"Abraham! Abraham!" . . . "I know that God is first in your life—you have not withheld even your beloved son from me" (Genesis 22:11, 12, *The Living Bible*).

Scripture: Genesis 22:9-18
Song: "All for Jesus"

Jim Elliot once said, "He is no fool who gives what he cannot keep to gain what he cannot lose." In early 1956, Jim and four other missionaries to Equador were martyred for their faith by the Auca Indians.

In laying the groundwork for their mission, the five families established a mission compound before searching for Auca villages, using Nate Saint's plane. They found one village and made contact with the people, dropping gifts and messages into the village from the plane. The gifts were received, and several gifts expressing friendship were returned. Soon they received permission from the Aucas to land on Palm Beach, an island in the Curray River. There they met several Aucas and were encouraged by their response. On January 8, Jim radioed his wife, Elisabeth, saying they were going into the village and that they would report back three hours later.

When there was no message, Elisabeth and the other wives contacted the authorities. They found the five men brutally murdered at their campsite. These men had given the ultimate sacrifice of their lives in service to the Lord Jesus Christ.

Father, may I be willing to give my all in Your service as Jim Elliot and many other martyrs of the faith have done in the past. I desire to live out my faith before others, relinquishing all I have to You, so that others see Christ in me. In Jesus' name, amen.

Transparent Living

We can plainly see that the LORD is with you. . . . Look how the LORD has blessed you! (Genesis 26:28, 29, *New Living Translation*).

Scripture: Genesis 26:26-31
Song: "I Am the Vine"

When I "grow up," I want to be like my mother. Oh, not in her looks, necessarily. Nor even with all her health problems, though I have inherited a few of those. But in her heart's desire: that Christ would be seen in her.

Many times I've been with her when someone came and thanked her for reflecting Christ. I believe many will be in Heaven because of the way she lived her life. She sought Him every day, beginning her day early in His Word and prayer. (She was a nurse and often worked the 7-3 day shift). She truly believed that for her to live meant Christ alone. As a result, she overflowed with love for Him and His Word—a love that she passed down to her three children and many others.

The apostle Paul's prayer for the Colossians was the prayer of my mom's heart: ""We continually ask God to fill you with the knowledge of his will through all the wisdom and understanding that the Spirit gives, so that you may live a life worthy of the Lord and please him in every way: bearing fruit in every good work, growing in the knowledge of God" (1:9, 10). This is now my desire too.

Father in Heaven, my heart's desire is that others see Christ in me. It doesn't come easily, for in learning more of Christ, I must enter into His life of suffering. But drawing others to You—by His life lived in me—is worth it all. I pray this prayer in the name of Jesus, my merciful Savior and Lord. Amen.

Reward of Obedience

Do as I say. . . . If you do, I will be with you and bless you (Genesis 26:2, 3, *The Living Bible*).

Scripture: Genesis 21:12-14, 17-21; 26:2-5, 12, 13
Song: "There Shall Be Showers of Blessing"

"Obedience is the very best way to show that you believe," my young daughter warbled joyfully, as she went out to play. "Doing exactly what the Lord commands."

I stood inside the screen door watching her and shaking my head. Not at the truth she was singing but at how quickly and glibly it poured out. Especially as she had just been disciplined for disobedience. Obviously, our talk on what obedience looked like triggered the song she'd heard and sung many times before.

As she went on into the chorus, spelling out the word *obedience*, the thought crossed my mind that I was no better than she was when it came to my obedience to the Lord. Could others see through my actions to my reluctance at times to obey? Did they see the avoidance measures, the "exception clauses" I created in order to look good in my disobedience?

God reminded me that day that while He demands my obedience, He also blesses His children who do what He says. As I listened to one of His greatest blessings to me (my daughter) finish the song, I recommitted to obeying my heavenly Father . . . right away. With joy.

Father, I'm reminded that I need to learn obedience. Even Your perfect, spotless Son had to learn this lesson through His suffering. But You have also promised that when I have learned it, You will shower me with Your blessings. Thank You for Your faithfulness and goodness. In Your holy name I pray. Amen.

Insatiable Quest for Guidance

Everyone who drinks this water will be thirsty again, but whoever drinks the water I give them will never thirst (John 4:13, 14).

Scripture: John 4:1-15
Song: "We're Feeding on the Living Bread"

A young mother of three was debating with friends about the kind of discipline she should use with her 6-year-old daughter. The little girl hadn't treated her younger sister respectfully, and Mom was frustrated with her behavior. She told the young girl that she was not allowed to have a birthday party with all of her friends, only with her family.

In the social media outlet the mother uses frequently, she asked her friends to comment on whether she had done the right thing. After several comments, the mother added that the young girl had already told her friends at school that she was having a party—and the friends were excited about celebrating her special day with her. Therefore, this mother felt as though she had already lost the battle and had no choice but to give in to the little girl.

In all of the comments that people shared, no one directed Mom to what God has to say about disciplining children. She couldn't find peace with her decisions from her friends. But if we allow God the opportunity, He will fill us with wisdom and peace.

Lord, when I am listening to the ramblings of others, may I run to You for guidance, understanding, and wisdom. In Jesus' name, amen.

October 21–27. **Dawn Cherie Olson** is an international business virtual professor and stewardship ministry leader. She writes about finances and relationships from Nashville, Tennessee.

Noting Preferences

Now, my son, listen carefully and do what I tell you: Go out to the flock and bring me two choice young goats, so I can prepare some tasty food for your father, just the way he likes it (Genesis 27:8, 9).

Scripture: Genesis 27:1-10
Song: "Come and Dine"

"All things are ready, come to the feast." As a traditional southern family, we knew that food is the center of socializing in the home. There was never an event, holiday, celebration, or death that didn't involve massive amounts of food.

The most important of these meals for our family was Sunday dinner. As a young girl learning to prepare the meals, I was taught how my father preferred his food. I followed my mother's ways, and I watched the pleasure of a well-cooked meal shine in my father's eyes as he savored each and every bite.

As a child, though I wasn't skilled enough to prepare those fried chicken dinners, I'd rummage around in the refrigerator looking for the cold cuts for Dad's sandwich. I would serve him a sandwich with just the right amount of tomato, crisp lettuce, and bologna—on a plate with a napkin gently tucked underneath. He'd be listening to the Kentucky Wildcats game over the radio in his dusky office and always welcomed my tasty interruptions.

Bringing something pleasing to him made me feel loved and appreciated. Isn't it that way with the heavenly Father too?

Lord, may I prepare for You in a way that is pleasing to Your eyes and heart. Please guide me in my kingdom work. In Jesus' name, amen.

Under the Disguise

Then Rebekah took the best clothes of Esau her older son, which she had in the house, and put them on her younger son Jacob. She also covered his hands and the smooth part of his neck with the goatskins (Genesis 27:15, 16).

Scripture: Genesis 27:11-17
Song: "Remove My Covering, Lord"

As my daughter approached her first Halloween, we read books about finding costumes, trick-or-treating, and the disguises that people wear for fun. She seemed excited about the holiday, and I felt I had adequately prepared her for it.

We started with the fall festival at church where they were hosting a "trunk-or-treat." It was during the early evening, and she had so much fun walking up to the decorated cars filled with candy. We arrived home at dusk, and my husband joyfully prepared to take her trick-or-treating. She held his hand tightly as the many children raced from house to house, asking for their treats. After a few minutes, she was running too and having a great time.

The best part of Halloween, of course, is simply recalling that the word is short for "All Hallow's Eve" in the traditional church year. It's the day before what is often refered to All Saints' Day, when we remember loved ones and Christian martyrs who have gone on before us.

Lord, let us recognize Your graceful presence in all things, and give us clear vision to see past others' disguises. And may we be assured that nothing can cover us from Your view and Your love. In Jesus' name, amen.

A Unique Scent

So he went to him and kissed him. When Isaac caught the smell of his clothes, he blessed him and said, "Ah, the smell of my son is like the smell of a field that the LORD has blessed" (Genesis 27:27).

Scripture: Genesis 27:18-29
Song: "Christ, from Whom All Blessings Flow"

How exciting to prepare for the arrival of a child! One of the most rewarding times for me, as a mother, was sorting all of the baby clothes. After washing those new baby clothes, I opened the dryer, and the aroma of baby detergent filled the air.

I breathed deeply and took in all of the sweet smells of the clean, new clothes. Being highly sensitive to scents during pregnancy, this was a welcome change.

I folded each of the little outfits and placed them gently in the drawers. My mom had always said to put a bar of scented soap in your drawers to keep the clothes smelling fresh, and I had chosen some lightly fragrant ones for my daughter's dresser.

I was ready for her little sweetness to arrive. But once she came into our lives, her sweet smell often collided with the foul odor of used diapers and spit-up!

So, my laundry pile was large, but each time I opened the dryer, the aroma of the baby detergent would once again fill the air. Except now, the clothes also had her scent, unique and wonderful to me.

Lord, may we savor the gentle reminders of Your presence through the natural aromas of Your world. Help us to appreciate all things that You have created in their own uniqueness. Through Christ I pray. Amen.

Ongoing Battle—for "Stuff"?

Your name will no longer be Jacob, but Israel, because you have struggled with God and with humans and have overcome (Genesis 32:28).

Scripture: Genesis 32:22-30
Song: "Fight the Battle in the Body"

In my professional life, I've had many adventures that were generally driven by financial need. My first jobs were the typical teenager jobs: video store, pizza place, hamburger and ice cream shop, and franchise restaurants. During those times, I was beginning to earn my own money and discover what it was like to be "independently wealthy."

In the decade that followed, I began training and searching for jobs that would further my financial well-being. And during this whole time, I battled with God about what I was supposed to have and how I was supposed to get it. My problem was that I so often sacrificed family, friends, and coworkers to forward my own agenda. I was once in a lawsuit over a $12 late fee for video rentals.

Through all of these battles, I did not prepare. I had no armor, no vision of the goal, and no strategy. I was financially driven to obtain the things "society" seemed to tell me I needed. I had far more than most at an early age. And yet, I selfishly held on to my stuff. During the 10 years after that, I began to lose my stuff and recognize that what God provided was more than enough.

Lord, may I begin each day by cloaking myself in Your armor. Guide me through each trial with Your wisdom. Though I may not always know how I will get through, I ask that You strengthen me by prayer and the Word. In Christ, amen.

A Sacred Place

Jacob set up a stone pillar at the place where God had talked with him, and he poured out a drink offering on it; he also poured oil on it (Genesis 35:14).

Scripture: Genesis 35:9-15
Song: "Hush! Blessed Are the Dead"

Jean slowly walked through the cemetery, arm in arm with her two daughters. They were visiting the family grave site to place flowers around her husband's resting place. It was nearly two years ago, on this day, when she had heard the news from the doctor that it was time to "make him comfortable" at home. They had ordered the appropriate hospital bed and walkers, but she wasn't sure how much time she had with him.

When they brought him home, she turned on his favorite John Wayne movie and sat near him. He couldn't talk much, but he gently squeezed her hand when she reached out to him. Three months later, he passed away in his sleep.

Jean wandered around and looked at the places around their home that she wouldn't change. Although her health was failing too, she wanted to honor her husband and the life they had shared together. She gave away all of his clothes and shoes, but she left his hats hanging neatly on the hall stand, right where he left them. In the beautiful rolling hills of the Kentucky countryside, she knelt down. Laying the flowers gently next to the headstone, she ran her fingers over his engraved name and prayed.

God of all the saints, living and dead, may I honor You in this sacred place where You have spoken with me. May I be still and listen as You bless me with Your grace and mercy. In the holy name of Jesus, my Lord and Savior, I pray. Amen.

A New Land

The LORD will be my God and this stone that I have set up as a pillar will be God's house, and of all that you give me I will give you a tenth (Genesis 28:21, 22).

Scripture: Genesis 28:1, 10-22
Song: "God Has Set the Land Before Us"

Bryson had been packing for weeks to move to their new apartment. Though he'd been actively looking for jobs, he hadn't yet received an offer of employment. His mother called every day, trying to talk him out of moving to another state.

He was moving with his wife and their two small children. Cara had been a stay-at-home mom for several years now and was ready to return to work. As a result, she wanted to move close to her family for support. He could see the pain in her eyes and the longing for a fresh start.

Yet his mother and father couldn't understand this "leap of faith." Bryson believed God would provide for him and his family as long as he continued to be obedient. Yet how could he explain this faith to his family?

With significant anxiety, he called them and told about how many doors had been opened to him and his wife since they had decided to move. There was no denying that God had a guiding hand in their journey. As they sat on their new patio, he sighed with relief at the blessings that continued to come through for them.

O Lord, I praise You for all the blessings You've poured into my life down through the years. Today, help me recognize every good thing You provide— and lift up my heart in gratitude. In the name of the Father, the Son, and the Holy Spirit, I pray. Amen.

What Kind of Legacy?

Then a new king, to whom Joseph meant nothing, came to power in Egypt (Exodus 1:8).

Scripture: Exodus 1:7-14
Song: "Make Me a Blessing"

What child doesn't remember the story of Joseph, his colorful coat, and the dreams—oh yes, the dreams that came true. Joseph saw the sun, moon, and stars bowing down to him. And picture the lean cows eating up the fat ones in the Pharaoh's dreams. Through these dreams, Joseph was shown God's plan for his life.

God worked through Joseph to protect the lives of the Egyptians and the children of Israel. But even with Joseph's great accomplishments, there came a time when the kings of Egypt would remember him no more.

Do you ever wonder how you'll be remembered? Do you feel that someday your good deeds will be buried along with your body? As the years pass, I consider whether my life story will have any meaning for my children and grandchildren. Will the way I've lived my life influence them positively? I'm not sure, but today I'll take the time to look at my legacy and consider the effect of my deeds on God's work in the world. I want to be creating a "life story" that God will honor and remember, even if the world forgets.

Dear Father, today I examine my actions in the light of Your perfection. Help me to see where I'm pleasing You—and where I can improve. In Jesus' name, amen.

October 28–31. **Diane Gruchow** lives in the Colorado mountains with her husband of 50 years. She spends her time writing, mentoring single moms, and riding her horses.

Quiet Courage

The midwives, however, feared God and did not do what the king of Egypt had told them to do; they let the boys live (Exodus 1:17).

Scripture: Exodus 1:15-22
Song: "I Know Who Holds Tomorrow"

The young father ran back toward the house. His right sleeve was on fire, but he didn't even notice. "Help me, they're in there! Help me! My boys!" He shattered the door with his burning arm and threw himself inside. His two little guys were huddled together by the bedroom door. The man lifted them from the inferno and ran.

Bravery comes in many forms. This Texas dad, who saved the lives of his children from their burning mobile home, demonstrated courage amidst extreme physical danger. But there's another type of courage that sometimes goes unnoticed. It's the quiet strength that we gain by depending upon the Holy Spirit to guide our actions.

Recently I hurt a friend and needed to apologize for my actions. But I was afraid she might reject my attempt to make things right. Through prayer, God gave me the courage to call her, and our relationship was mended. It seems such a small thing now, but facing even one of those everyday fears becomes a big hurdle to jump if we try to do it without God's help.

Dear Lord, may I have the courage to give You every one of my fears, to place them in Your beautiful, strong hands. Sometimes I feel so afraid of what this life will bring, but I do truly believe that You are king over all. You control everything that I fear. Thank You, my Father, in Jesus' name. Amen.

Are You Watching?

When she could hide him no longer, she got a papyrus basket for him and coated it with tar and pitch. Then she placed the child in it and put it among the reeds along the bank of the Nile. His sister stood at a distance to see what would happen to him (Exodus 2:3, 4).

Scripture: Exodus 2:1-10
Song: "How Strong and Sweet My Father's Care"

The clock ticks its seconds, one by one. The sun begins to rise in the gray morning sky, and all the while I watch and wait. I watch to see what's happening in the forest around me. Are the tiny new rabbits safe? Is the young coyote still around? Will I see deer this morning?

Waiting and watching can bring us a sense of calm and peace. But sometimes the specters of fear or pain march along with those waiting ticks of the clock. So often, our watching is more important than my early morning musing. Sometimes it involves weightier matters.

Moses' sister was on guard duty. She was making sure that he would be safe. You can be certain that, if there was danger, she would rescue him. But for now, she was *watching* and *waiting*.

Sometimes it's all we can do, and it's hard. You may be waiting to see if that wayward child will see the light and come back to God. You may be watching over a seriously ill loved one. These are painful things, but remember, God is watching too.

Father God, I know You see everything in my life, and You love me so much that my waiting and watching touches Your heart. Help me to feel Your presence while I wait and to know that You have my whole world in Your hands. In Jesus' name, amen.

No Longer a Stranger

Zipporah gave birth to a son, and Moses named him Ger-shom, saying, "I have become a foreigner in a foreign land" (Exodus 2:22).

Scripture: Exodus 2:15-25
Song: "I'm But a Stranger Here"

My grandfather, Gustav, immigrated to the United States from Lithuania as a young man. Honest and upright, he worked hard to develop his land and became respected by his neighbors as a diligent man, true to his word. However, within a few years, things changed.

A world war caused uncertainty, anger, and uneasiness among the people. Those same neighbors, whose respect he had earned, turned against him. Since Gustav and his family spoke German in their home, they were suspect, and he was now viewed as an alien, even an enemy in his adopted land.

Neighbors conjured up lies about him. The FBI searched his barns for anything that would tie him to Germany. His wife and children suffered name-calling and other abuse. No longer accepted, he truly became a stranger in a foreign land.

When you feel like a stranger in your world, don't despair. If you claim Jesus as your Savior, you belong. You belong to the Creator of the universe. You are God's child, and that's a pretty impressive lineage. You're no longer a stranger, but a member of the family cherished and valued by God, your Father.

My loving Father, thank You for making me part of Your family. Sometimes I feel like a stranger in this world; I don't always fit. But God, please help me remember that I do belong to You. In Your Son's name I ask this. Amen.

DEVOTIONS®

> Who among the gods is like you, LORD? Who is
> like you—majestic in holiness, awesome in glory,
> working wonders?
>
> —*Exodus 15:11.*

Gary Wilde, Editor   **Margaret Williams,** Project Editor   Photo © Hemera | Thinkstock®

God Doesn't Cover His Eyes

When they heard that the LORD was concerned about them and had seen their misery, they bowed down and worshiped (Exodus 4:31).

Scripture: Exodus 4:27-31
Song: "Somebody Cares"

After the car accident that almost took the life of her husband, Shirley sat by his bedside watching his chest rise and fall. She watched as he groaned in pain and struggled for breath. Day after day, she watched and prayed and, at times, she just covered her eyes. She didn't want to see him this way.

Looking at someone in great pain hurts, doesn't it? And the hurt is compounded many times over when we love that person dearly. I wonder if God hurts when He sees the misery and pain in this world. I wonder if He wishes that He didn't have to see it, especially since He loves us so completely.

The Scripture says that He saw the misery of His people and was concerned about them. In 2 Corinthians 1:3, the Bible describes God as "the Father of compassion and the God of all comfort." What a warm feeling it gives me to know of God's compassion for all of His people.

So when we're in pain, whether physical or emotional, we can be assured that the "God of all comfort" is watching. He's not hiding His eyes. He looks on our pain and comforts us in love.

Father, there is so much hurt and pain around me, but I know how much You care for Your people. So I praise and worship You for Your love. In Jesus' name, amen.

November 1–3. **Diane Gruchow** lives in the Colorado Mountains with her husband of 50 years. She spends her time writing, mentoring single moms, and riding her horses.

Take Off Your Sandals

"**Do not come any closer,**" God said. "**Take off your sandals, for the place where you are standing is holy ground**" (Exodus 3:5).

Scripture: Exodus 3:1-6
Song: "We Are Standing on Holy Ground"

The old Marine tried to stand at attention while the flag was passing by. It was difficult for him to raise his body out of his wheelchair, but he would allow himself no excuses. He would stand, and he would salute. This flag was the symbol of the country he loved, respected, and had fought for.

A woman sitting next to him tried to help but didn't have the strength. As a young man walked by, he saw the struggle. He saw the tears beginning to form in the old Marine's eyes, and he stopped, lifted the old man to a standing position, and removed his own baseball cap. The people around them noticed what was happening and, one by one, stood in silent respect for this soldier and the symbol of the country he loved.

God told Moses to show respect, to take off his sandals. This was holy ground. God was there, and respect for the awesome king of the universe was clearly demanded. It's worship, and worship is all about giving God the respect due Him in His presence. As I think of my Master, my God—as I try to do His will, and as I pray to Him—I'm standing on holy ground, always in His presence.

My Father, I praise Your name. Thank You for the example of Moses, his life and desire to serve You. May You smile at my small efforts to show the respect You deserve. Because Jesus opened the door to your throne room, I pray. Amen.

He Sees That Pink Pumpkin!

Moses said to God, "Who am I that I should go to Pharaoh and bring the Israelites out of Egypt?" And God said, "I will be with you" (Exodus 3:11, 12).

Scripture: Exodus 3:7-17
Song: "My God, Accept My Heart This Day"

God answered Moses with these words, "I will be with you." It's interesting to me that the Lord didn't try to talk Moses out of his lack of confidence. Maybe that tells us something.

When my child proudly hands me a drawing of a pink circle with three black dots, I'd better be a little careful what I say. If I pretend to understand his rough drawing and say, "It looks just like you," he may burst into tears, and I will have forfeited the trust he had in me. (Or at the very least, he will wonder at my poor eyesight!)

Couldn't I recognize that this was a pink pumpkin? I don't help him by pretending to understand his picture, and God doesn't pretend either. He knows our abilities and wants us to use them.

If there is something God asks us to do, we can trust Him to know what can be accomplished with our abilities and to bridge any difficulties. So, if God asks you to speak to Pharaoh—or to a group of teens or to your neighbor—you can be sure that He knows your limitations, and that He will recognize the "pink pumpkin" of your efforts. God didn't tell Moses, "You can do it." He told Moses, and He tells us, "I will be with you."

My Father, today I will do my best to paint a beautiful picture for You. Please help me see my abilities and inabilities with Your eyes. In Jesus' name, amen.

Early Morning

Jesus walked by. John looked at him intently and then declared, "See! There is the Lamb of God!" (John 1:36, *The Living Bible*).

Scripture: John 1:29-37
Song: "Behold the Glories of the Lamb"

The earth is hard under my feet. A frosty, chilly morning alerts me to summer's end. The sweet smell of sagebrush fills the air as I walk a mile trying to maintain a steady pace.

Along the mountain trail, I come to a standstill. A heavy mist blankets the valley below while distant mountain peaks seem to burst above the fog, moisture hanging like teardrops under the foliage.

Then a single ray of sun, shining through the droplets, creates a myriad of color—a tiny rainbow. *God is near.* I can feel His presence walking with me. When I arrive at the bridge, I know I'm at my halfway point. Gazing up the river, I look to the heavens and say, "Lord, wash over me, as the river washes over the rocks below. In this beautiful moment, please cleanse me!"

It's a habit now—this morning walk with Jesus. When I look at the sky, I realize without a shadow of a doubt that He is my redeemer, "The Lamb of God, who takes away the sin of the world" (John 1:29).

Lord, why am I in such a hurry? I wonder how many times You pass me by and I don't notice? Don't allow me to miss a moment with You. Help me be more aware of Your constant presence. In the name of Jesus, I pray. Amen.

November 4–10. **Shirley Reynolds** is a freelance writer living in a rural community in the mountains of Idaho. Besides writing, one of her passions is riding her 4-wheeler through the back country.

He Answers: But How and When?

Moses went back to the LORD. "LORD," he protested, "How can you mistreat your own people like this? Why did you ever send me, if you were going to do this to them?" (Exodus 5:22, *The Living Bible*).

Scripture: Exodus 5:19-23
Song: "Wherever He Leads I'll Go"

Listening intently to an account of the murders of Korean orphans, I asked God, "How can anyone harm innocent children? Why, Lord, do you allow these things to happen?"

When the conference speaker was finished, she asked: "Will you please pick up a wooden cross from the front table, as a reminder to pray for abused children around the world?"

I was tired from attending classes all day at the Colorado Christian Writer's conference, but I took a cross and held it in my hand. Heading out the door into the chilly night air, I walked to my room.

"Lord," I said, "I don't understand why children have to die!"

When I stepped into my room, I looked through my window at the snowcapped peaks of the Rockies, and I stood and prayed. "O God, I know that in all things, You work for the good, and that even amidst great evil, there is hope for redemption. But it's so hard for me to grasp."

I felt like Moses, who speaks in our Scripture today. I know God will answer me—but I still don't know how, I still don't know when.

God, I know that while we live in this world, bad things will happen. I put my hope in that day when You make all things right by Your omnipotent power. In Christ, amen.

His Power: to Thunder . . . to Care

I am Jehovah, the Almighty God who appeared to Abraham, Isaac, and Jacob—though I did not reveal my name, Jehovah, to them (Exodus 6:2, 3, *The Living Bible*).

Scripture: Exodus 6:2-9
Song: "How Majestic Is Your Name"

The words *Father, God, Jehovah,* and *Almighty* reveal a stronger, higher power than any of us. There are times, though, when I forget that awesome majesty in the busyness of my life.

My father used to say that every time it thundered, it meant that the angels were bowling. But one night, when my grandson was staying with us in our mountain cabin, we experienced a horrific storm. Trying not to show my fear, I watched the lightning flash across the sky. Yet when the thunder crashed, rattling the windows, I trembled.

My grandson and I watched, while I tried to comfort him. Ponderosa Pines swayed back and forth, and the wind blew branches and pine needles across our deck. I started to say, "That's quite a bowling game in Heaven," when 7-year-old Mikie looked at me and said, "Come on, Grandma, don't be afraid—it's just a storm."

I thought about his comment and God's awesome power displayed in this frightening thunderstorm. The Lord is so much bigger than I could ever understand. Then I felt a little hand on my shoulder. "Don't worry, Grandma; God will take care of us."

My awesome Heavenly Father, help me to see Your wonder in simple things and not question Your intent in my life. Help me to accept Your mighty power and majesty in all things—even in Your ability to take care of me. Through Christ I pray. Amen.

Wasn't It a Miracle?

The LORD had told Moses, "Pharaoh won't listen, and this will give me the opportunity of doing mighty miracles to demonstrate my power" (Exodus 11:9, *The Living Bible*).

Scripture: Exodus 11
Song: "Under His Wings"

As God told Moses that "Pharaoh won't listen, and this will give me the opportunity of doing mighty miracles," I've wondered, *Do we expect miracles today?*

A blood clot in my brain put me in a coma for three days. Even while asleep, I heard every word between the doctor and my family. Evidently, the doctors didn't believe I would survive.

Thankfully, God had another plan. In my comatose dreams, I walked down a narrow path with Jesus and begged Him to let me live and tell others about Him. I wanted to write.

Jesus walked with me, and then I awakened. It was Sunday morning, and it took awhile for me to open my eyes and realize that I had indeed survived. My first request was, "Please call my husband!"

In my humble opinion, God performed a miracle in my life. But I've wondered since, "Did the hospital staff see a miracle in my awakening?"

"There will be side effects," the doctors had said—but there were none. I've wondered about the nurse who took my blood each day. What did she think when I opened my eyes . . . and she screamed?

Lord, thanks for the miracle of salvation by grace. Help me live in such a way that I'll always expect miracles to happen, large and small. In Jesus' name, amen.

All Through the Years

Your children ask, "What does all this mean? What is this ceremony about?" (Exodus 12:26, *The Living Bible*).

Scripture: Exodus 12:21-28
Song: "God's Word Is Our Great Heritage"

"Daddy, why do you tell me stories about the church, the Bible, and God?" I asked.

"Because God wants us to pass these stories on to our families and friends," he said. "Then you can tell them to your own children some day."

I've thought about my heritage. I was raised in the church from birth. I've thought about special people in my life, who have passed on tidbits of truth to me, and in turn, I've passed those stories on to my children and my grandson.

My family used to spend part of each summer at our local church camp meeting, parking our trailer on a site we'd purchased. Evening services were held beneath a canvas tent with a carpet of straw, and there a certain tall Texas preacher made a lasting impact on my life—Dr. B. V. Seals. He had a booming voice, and I was captivated with his stories.

My father repeated many camp meeting stories to me as I sat on his lap before bedtime. When I asked my father, "Why do people go to the altar?" His answer was, "God meets you there. He forgives your sins and He loves you." The words spoken by great evangelists—and the words spoken by my own father—have stayed with me all through the years.

Father, may I never forget the times when I've felt You were so near me. Remind me to share those experiences with other people too. In Jesus' name, amen.

A Church Choir Miracle

The people of Israel followed all of Jehovah's instructions to Moses and Aaron (Exodus 12:50, *The Living Bible*).

Scripture: Exodus 12:43-51
Song: "The Blood Will Never Lose Its Power"

One morning I felt as if God were instructing me to "Assemble the church choir and go to Memory's bedside and perform the Easter musical!"

"You want us to perform the musical at a hospital?" Had this indeed been the Holy Spirit's nudging? My friend, Memory, was dying of brain cancer. And I know that her one great wish was to hear the Easter musical before she died.

I made a few calls, and eight choir members arrived at the hospital. With God's help, we performed the entire cantata for a dying friend.

We sang with gusto. Memory smiled, with tears flowing down her cheeks. When we finished, she hugged each one of us and said, "Thank you for making my wish come true!" Her family was seated in the hallway, and her son walked into the room weeping. He hugged me, and said, "There is nothing more you could have done to give her happiness—except what you did today. Thank you!"

As we walked from her room, we saw doctors and nurses quietly clapping. They lined the hallway. It was then I knew God had orchestrated more than just the music. Later that afternoon, Memory went to be with the Lord.

Dear Father, help me listen closely, each day, for Your still, small voice. Let me never miss an opportunity to follow Your instructions! In Jesus' name, amen.

Ready for the Lord's Visit?

This is how you are to eat it: with your cloak tucked into your belt, your sandals on your feet and your staff in your hand. Eat it in haste; it is the Lord's Passover (Exodus 12:11).

Scripture: Exodus 12:1-14
Song: "Since Jesus Passed By"

Dad lived his life as if each day were his last. In his later years, he often said he was "ready to go home." When he suffered a severe stroke, his care became my responsibility.

He was hardly able to speak, but we walked the aisles of the care center, and I talked to him about my life. He loved to sit in the courtyard, but in his small room, he sat in his own rocking chair. In the midst of my conversations with him, he would walk over to the window, gaze up at the sky, and lose himself in his own thoughts. Every now and then he'd cry.

I held his hands and thought about all the things Dad had taught me through the years. "Always be ready to go," he'd say. "Never lay your head on your pillow, unless you are ready."

I've thought about those words since and try to make each day count for God. Some days I may not accomplish a whole lot—but I know all my days are blessed with God's presence. When Dad passed away, he left this earth but he also left me a heritage beyond value. When I feel distressed over some problem, I often remember his words: "Be ever ready!"

O Eternal Lord God, show me how to be ready at all times for Your direction. Help me to have my traveling clothes on—to be prepared—and ready to go with my walking stick. I don't want to miss Your visit. In the holy name of Jesus, my Lord and Savior, I pray. Amen.

Intentional Living

Let the Holy Spirit guide your lives. Then you won't be doing what your sinful nature craves (Galatians 5:16, *New Living Translation*).

Scripture: Galatians 5:13-21
Song: "Draw Me Close"

While we were shopping, my 3-year-old daughter found a pocket sewing kit. Oblivious to the hazardous needles, she focused on the bright thread and sparkly buttons. Excitedly she asked if she could have it. I explained to her what it was, told her no, and moved on.

We had made our purchases and had buckled ourselves in the car when I noticed she was being oddly quiet. "What are you holding?" I asked. Very slowly she pulled the little sewing kit out from her coat. "I really wanted it, Mama."

I could see that my daughter was in great turmoil. Something inside her knew it was wrong, yet she wanted it so badly. My first thought: *I can't believe my child is a shoplifter!* My second thought: *We are all born sinners — and this is a teachable moment.* The lesson unfolded as we returned to the store.

Because sin is natural to us, our struggles will never get easier until we surrender control to the Holy Spirit. Yet, as we lay down our own desires, we realize that all we really need is Him.

Father, my deepest desire is to live by the power of the Holy Spirit, but I am a work in progress, and I know You don't expect perfection in my Christian growth. Thankfully, the perfection came in the work of Jesus on the cross. Through Him I pray. Amen.

November 11–17. **Tami Lambertson** was born and raised in the Midwest. She is a freelance writer and licensed minister.

The Little Things

In the future, your children will ask you, "What does all this mean?" Then you will tell them, "With the power of his mighty hand, the LORD brought us out of Egypt, the place of our slavery" (Exodus 13:14, *New Living Translation*).

Scripture: Exodus 13:11-16
Song: "He Saved Us to Show His Glory"

As a stay-at-home mother of three, I often babysit for a bit of extra cash. So it's common to have six or seven little ones gathered around the table for lunch. On one such occasion, I reminded one of our guests not to eat until we had prayed. With an incredulous look he blurted, "You pray in the daytime? We wait until we go to bed at our house!"

When the laughter subsided, my son seized the opportunity to explain how we choose to thank God for providing our food before we eat it. The rest of our dinner conversation revolved around the Lord, His Word, and His promises to us. That simple act of praying became a witness to God's goodness.

My approach to everyday situations should be a testimony of His faithfulness. Telling others about what Jesus has done isn't a presentation; it's simply part of an ongoing conversation. It's the little things—things I might not give a second thought to—that provide such immense opportunities to speak of the Lord to tell about all He has done for us.

O God, the King of glory, thank You that I am no longer a slave to sin. As I quietly live for You, let my actions shout the difference in my life, because of Your goodness and grace toward me. When curious souls begin to question, may I be quick to give You the glory. In Jesus' name I pray. Amen.

You Are My Light

The LORD went ahead of them. He guided them during the day with a pillar of cloud, and he provided light at night with a pillar of fire (Exodus 13:21, *New Living Translation*).

Scripture: Exodus 13:17-22
Song: "Lead Me, Lord"

The hour was late. I was lost. Without much choice, I decided to keep following the confident voice of my car's GPS. My stomach was in knots as I made turn after turn, driving deeper into some rough-looking neighborhoods of a huge city. I knew I would reach my last stop, but the current route seemed to have no outlet. And . . . this definitely wasn't a place to get out and ask for directions, so I just kept looking into the distance for signs.

Finally, I turned onto a main avenue and, within half a block, arrived at my desired destination. Before venturing anywhere else, I changed the settings on the navigation system from "shortest route" to "fastest time" to avoid the back roads in this unfamiliar territory.

I'm so grateful the Lord promises to be my guide, just as He guided His people through the desert so long ago. I can depend on Him to lead the way, even in the darkest hour, through the scariest situations. If I make a wrong turn or get off course, I can get back on track by allowing His Word to light my path and by listening for the confident whispers to my heart.

Father, I know You might not take me through on the "fastest time," but You guarantee I'll reach my destination. You truly know what's best for me, so thank You for being my light and guiding me. Help me to trust the directions You give. Lead me, Lord, in Jesus' name. Amen.

Hot Pursuit

The Egyptians chased after them with all the forces in Pharaoh's army—all his horses and chariots, his charioteers, and his troops (Exodus 14:9, *New Living Translation*).

Scripture: Exodus 14:5-9
Song: "Power of Your Love"

Several years ago, Charlotte was diagnosed with a chronic illness. With no known cause and no known cure, she was depending on God to heal her body. Eventually, Charlotte had no choice but to check into the hospital until her flare-up was under control.

The initial news was devastating: she had no medical coverage for her preexisting condition. All her summer plans came to a screeching halt. *Why did this have to happen now?* Between the pain and an uncertain future, Charlotte felt the *enemy* known as discouragement closing in.

Nevertheless, Charlotte put her faith in high gear. She decided that if she was going to be confined to a bed, it wasn't going to be wasted time. What the enemy meant for harm, God would use for good. Instead of looking at the problem, she looked at those around her. Charlotte made the most of every opportunity and shared God's love with all who entered her room.

The way Charlotte walked through her trial proved the old adage, "The greater the test, the greater the testimony." In moments of life when you feel chased by every adversary, look to Jesus. He has a bigger plan in mind.

Dear Heavenly Father, thank You for Your constant protection. I know that whatever I face, it is covered by the power of Your love. In Jesus' name, amen.

Remain Calm

The LORD himself will fight for you. Just stay calm (Exodus 14:14, *New Living Translation*).

Scripture: Exodus 14:10-14
Song: "I Don't Need Anything but You"

The bills piled up, and Adam and Julia were in a real mess. Since their daughter's surgery, they just couldn't seem to catch up. Yet the couple was determined to make ends meet on one income; that would keep Julia home with their young brood.

However, she was growing tired of the lifestyle of sacrifice. God had given her two hands and a solid work ethic—wasn't it time to put them to use?

As she browsed the classifieds for opportunities, her son approached. "Mommy, when I go to Heaven, can I give Jesus a hug?" Julia pulled the child near for a conversation about the person of Jesus, His love, and His closeness to them. In her attempt to teach her boy, she received encouragement of her own. Julia threw away the newspaper with a renewed sense of hope that God's faithfulness never ends.

When facing our enemies, it's hard to see the face of the Lord. We strategize about how to take care of a problem, thinking we can fix things quicker and easier. Being still has the appearance of doing nothing. But often the act of being still or remaining calm requires more wisdom and discipline than immediately attempting to repair things on our own.

Heavenly Father, help me to look to You in the midst of the battles of Christian growth. As I remain calm, You will fight the fight. Let me not grow weary or impatient, knowing that Your plan is always the best. In Christ's name I pray. Amen.

Just Wishin' and Whinin'?

Then the LORD said to Moses, "Why are you crying out to me? Tell the people to get moving!" (Exodus 14:15, *New Living Translation*).

Scripture: Exodus 14:15-20
Song: "The Great Adventure"

Last summer Tiffany learned to ride her bike without training wheels. She could zip around the block, ride over to a friend's house, and leave everyone in the dust as she sped by. Her new-found freedom was obvious to all and envied by her little brother, Darin. "She never waits for me! She always goes too fast! I can't do it!" It wasn't that he wanted her to wait for him, but he wanted to feel the rush of wind as she did, to pedal faster and go farther than he ever had before. He sat on the curb just a-wishin' and a-whinin'.

"If you want to keep up, then learn to ride your bike," his mother suggested. The next day, Darin was on a mission. He didn't give up; he believed he could do it. After a couple hours of sweat, frustration, and skinned knees, he raced his sister down the block. With unmatched elation he put his face into the wind.

Serving the Lord isn't always comfortable. Hard work, frustration, and the risk of getting hurt are part of the package. But we can't put our faith into action until we get up and move. Once we stop wishin' and whinin', we can start believin' and receivin'.

Dear Heavenly Father, help me get up and move by faith. As I step out, I believe You will prepare the way. Thank You for giving me the strength and courage to move forward to receive all You have planned for me. In Jesus' name, amen.

～ Just One ～

The waters returned and covered all the chariots and charioteers—the entire army of Pharaoh. Of all the Egyptians who had chased the Israelites into the sea, not a single one survived (Exodus 14:28, *New Living Translation*).

Scripture: Exodus 14:21-30
Song: "Faith Is the Victory"

I will never forget the day my mother was diagnosed with breast cancer. With one phone call her life flipped upside down. After radical surgery, her doctor told us that everything looked great, and he was sure they'd removed all abnormal cells.

The celebration, however, was short-lived. Upon further examination of the tissue, he discovered a micro-tumor that would need further testing. The positive result meant extra chemotherapy and more surgery. Lymph nodes that are next to malignant tumors are often removed because, if even one cancerous cell gets into those channels, the disease will likely return. It is the most common way cancer spreads. Due to the doctor's meticulous procedures and my mother's unwavering faith, today she is cancer free.

Just as it only takes a single cancer cell to destroy a human body, it only takes a single sin to destroy your soul. The good news is: the Lord has already fought that battle and won. We can live in victory instead of sickening with sin. God wiped out Egypt's entire army with the waters of the Red Sea, and Jesus wiped out sin and death with the atonement of the cross.

Father, my soul was dying with the disease of sin, and the prescription was the blood of Your Son. I am in awe of Your mercy and grace. In Christ's name, amen.

Given, Not Taken

Everyone who is willing is to bring to the LORD an offering (Exodus 35:5).

Scripture: Exodus 35:4-9
Song: "Take My Life and Let It Be"

My 2-year-old daughter, Zephani, is learning how to share. Whenever there is an extra toy, cookie, or chair, we show her how important it is to let others use our things. Most of the time, she understands and shares happily. However, my older children have found a sure way to rile her up. Instead of asking her to share, they snatch her things away. This violation of her personal space and dominion always results in a howl of protest.

It isn't that she is unwilling to share. It isn't that she needs or even wants all the toys to herself. It's just that there's a big difference between sharing and having things taken away.

Sharing requires a willing heart. When materials were needed to construct the tabernacle, Moses could have required items from each household. Demanding jewelry, thread, skins, and spices could have met the need. Certainly, a worship center for God's redeemed people was worth mandatory common sacrifice. Instead, God was pleased to build and furnish His tabernacle with offerings given willingly by enthusiastic worshippers. Offerings are given, not taken, and it still pleases God when worshippers willingly share their resources to honor Him.

Redeeming God, I marvel at Your generosity toward me. You gave lavishly and willingly to offer me forgiveness and eternal life. Thank You, in Jesus' name. Amen.

November 18–24. **Matthew Boardwell** is an avid nonfiction reader and enthusiastic musician. More importantly, he is husband to Pam, father of nine children, and a minister in Erie, Colorado.

Given with Skill

All who are skilled among you are to come and make everything the LORD has commanded (Exodus 35:10).

Scripture: Exodus 35:10-19
Song: "Give of Your Best to the Master"

In our church entrance hangs a beautiful painting encouraging everyone to delight in the corporate worship of God. The artwork is all the more inspiring once the artist's story is known.

"I turned to drawing and painting as an escape," Greg says. "It was a way for me to express my anger and sadness. Although I had an architecture degree, I really wanted to be an artist. I thought I could work in an architecture office during the day to support myself and at night experiment and improve my artwork. I really wanted to make a living at it." But when his dream career eluded him, in bitterness Greg turned to alcohol —and his artwork turned to blasphemy. The dark, brooding subjects he pursued mocked God and those whom God loves.

Then a coworker approached Greg with the gospel, highlighting Christ's forgiveness. Soon Greg placed his faith in Jesus, and his life changed forever. Now the beauty of his art brings glory to God. The same skill is focused in a new direction.

Moses invited anyone with a skill to employ it for God's glory. Seamstresses, goldsmiths, woodworkers, and tanners volunteered their talents to produce a corporate work of art, the tabernacle. However they used their skills before, now they were used for the Lord.

Father, I have used my gifts for many things, both good and bad. Help me to remember that the gifts You give can be given back to You in love. In Christ my Lord, Amen.

Giving Together

Everyone who was willing and whose heart moved them came and brought an offering to the LORD for the work on the tent of meeting (Exodus 35:21).

Scripture: Exodus 35:20-29
Song: "We Are God's People"

Once a month, our members show up at church with food in hand. A remarkable variety of foods—pasta salads, casseroles, roasts, cakes, and cobblers—line the counters in the kitchen adjacent to our worship space. The delicious aromas seep in throughout the service, making the mouth water even during the driest of sermons. The anticipation ends when we gather around the kitchen, offer thanks, and dig into our meal.

None of the dishes on that table makes a balanced meal by itself. And no single talented cook provided the variety we enjoy. Instead, *together* we indulge in the benefits of one another's talented cooking.

When the Israelites came together to build the tabernacle, they contributed diverse talents, abilities, and materials. Some brought their jewelry. Others donated fine wood. Still others gave spices. Each contribution was only a part. No single craftsman could lay claim to the whole accomplishment.

Churches still live this way today when members generously offer their own passions, skills, and resources together with others. This is how we build one another up for greater service.

Gracious Lord, by Your wisdom You created me with abilities and resources that can benefit others. Forgive me when I withhold them, and prompt me to give generously when my offering can help. All I have is Yours. In Christ's name I pray. Amen.

Spiritually Gifted to Give

The LORD has chosen Bezalel son of Uri, . . . and he has filled him with the Spirit of God, with wisdom, with understanding with knowledge and with all kinds of skills. And he has given [him] . . . the ability to teach others (Exodus 35:30, 31, 34).

Scripture: Exodus 35:30-35
Song: "We Give Thee but Thine Own"

When I worked construction the summer before my junior year of college, I was expected to show up with some tools of my own: hammer, tape measure, pencil, and utility knife in my own tool belt, the sort of standard tools that every construction worker needs to carry. But my boss assigned us a lot of tasks that those simple tools could not accomplish. For those assignments, we would rummage through his construction trailer. If the job required special tools, he provided them for us.

Bezalel is the first person in Scripture said to be filled with the Spirit. This filling was not merely for Bezalel's own benefit, but to equip him to accomplish the God-sized task of building the tabernacle. This assignment required special tools, so God provided them. Bezalel needed the inspiration of the Lord to do the artistic work of the Lord.

Christians have been assigned many tasks that are impossible without the spiritual gifts God provides. We show up for duty with our natural abilities and physical strength, but when special tools are needed, God provides them.

Spirit of God, I thank You for giving us all we need to do all You require. Help me recognize the spiritual gifts You have given me. Show me how and when to use them to do Your kingdom work. In Christ, amen.

Extraordinary Generosity

The people were restrained from bringing more, because what they already had was more than enough to do all the work (Exodus 36:6, 7).

Scripture: Exodus 36:2-7
Song: "Because I Have Been Given Much"

Normally, the Red Cross has a blood supply sufficient for only one to three days of ordinary hospital use. However, after the World Trade Center attacks of September 2001, Americans donated more blood than could be used up. But even though they had more than enough, Red Cross leaders couldn't bring themselves to announce it. They didn't want to discourage anyone from giving.

Can you imagine any charity organization calling a moratorium on fund drives? Can you imagine envelopes overflowing the sides of the offering plates and fluttering to the floor? Can you picture the offeratory music grinding to a halt halfway through as the minister urges people to stop giving? As hard as it is to imagine today, that is what happened when Moses asked Israel to contribute to the building of the tabernacle. The people were so enthusiastic about giving to that effort that the artisans were overwhelmed with materials.

How extraordinary it is when ministries have more than enough. That kind of giving takes extraordinary generosity, sacrifice, and faith.

O Lord my Shepherd, my cup overflows. You give me much more than I need. How delightful it would be if Your church and its ministries were supplied with more than enough! Grant me extraordinary faith to help make it happen. Through Jesus, amen.

Blessed for Giving

Moses inspected the work and saw that they had done it just as the LORD had commanded. So Moses blessed them (Exodus 39:43).

Scripture: Exodus 39:32-43
Song: "Something for Thee"

When a contractor purchases a building permit for a home, he agrees to a series of inspections. The foundation, framing, mechanical, and drywall all have to be examined carefully before the project progresses to the next stage. Each time an official signs the permit, it's a tribute to the diligence and expertise of the workers.

After all the officials have signed off and occupancy is approved, then comes the most important inspection of all. It's the final walk-through with the homeowners. Their response will indicate whether the contractor kept his promises. Theirs is the last word, the final assessment of a job well done . . . or not.

The artisans must have been watching Moses breathlessly as he scrutinized their work. Was the tabernacle worthy of the one who had commissioned it? For their generosity and diligence, they received the approval of Moses and the blessing of God.

Whenever we give or volunteer, let us keep in mind the "final inspection." At the final walk-through, our "work will be shown for what it is" (1 Corinthians 3:13). Will our life's work receive God's approval and blessing?

Blessed Father, I know my salvation comes through the work of Jesus alone. But You will reward the works I do, out of gratitude, in the power of Your Spirit. Teach me that my efforts for others are ultimately offerings to You. Through Christ, amen.

Glory Through Giving

Then the cloud covered the tent of meeting, and the glory of the LORD filled the tabernacle (Exodus 40:34).

Scripture: Exodus 40:16-30, 34, 38
Song: "Trust, Try, and Prove Me"

For a year our church prepared for a soccer skills camp outreach in the community. Some did the paperwork, approving the use of the fields. Others prepared Bible lessons for the kids who attended. Some arranged for food at the closing barbecue. Others bought the prizes to give away that night.

To staff the camp, a team of soccer players and their coach traveled from Missouri to Colorado. To host them, church families volunteered their spare bedrooms. Scores of kids showed up that week, learning soccer skills and Bible truths while having a lot of fun and making new friends.

During the closing barbecue, while I gave the talk, the supernatural hush of God's Spirit fell over the crowd. The simple gospel presentation brought tears to some eyes and repentance to one soul. Years later, that single decision to follow Jesus is still bearing fruit.

We applied all our resources, our skills, and our spiritual gifts, and God filled our completed work with His own glory. How gratifying it must have been for the whole community of Israel when God's glory filled the tabernacle!

Lord God Almighty, it is such a privilege to be part of Your church. Draw us together as we serve You. Help us recognize Your presence among us and fill us with Your glory. Guide us by Your Holy Spirit in all our work for You. I pray this prayer in the name of Jesus, my merciful Savior and Lord. Amen.

Made to Sing!

I will sing of the LORD's great love forever; with my mouth I will make your faithfulness known through all generations (Psalm 89:1).

Scripture: Psalm 89:1-7
Song: "All Praise to Thee, Eternal Lord"

You know the feeling, that moment when your heart sings! When I stand at the edge of the ocean at sunset or sit on a rock overlooking the mountains, or even when I walk the dog and look up at a full moon, my heart fills with song. *Yes, Lord, Your creation speaks!* Like the psalmist, I can say with all sincerity, "I will sing of the Lord's great love . . ." as I take in the overwhelming beauty here on earth. And I want to praise Him forever.

It doesn't matter whether I'm singing in tune or not, just as long as my heart, mind, and body take a moment to resonate with those holy ones who sing around the throne of God, day and night (see Revelation 5:6). And it doesn't matter whether I'm singing an ancient hymn or a recent praise song. Because of what Jesus Christ did for us on the cross, I can sing of God's love—forever. Not just now in my mortal body will I sing or even after other memories escape me in old age; I will sing in my new body in His presence forever.

Dear Lord, as a child, I thought that praising You in Heaven might be a boring way to spend eternity. But I'm beginning to understand. Like the psalmist, I was made to sing of Your love for eternity—while You give me work to do in Your kingdom come! All praise to You, in Jesus' name. Amen.

November 25–30. **Carol McLean** is digital products manager for ValPak in Naples, Florida. She lives with her husband on the gulf coast and enjoys the sunsets at beautiful Bonita Beach.

Who's the Leader?

I have found David my servant; with my sacred oil I have anointed him. My hand will sustain him; surely my arm will strengthen him (Psalm 89:20, 21).

Scripture: Psalm 89:19-24
Song: "Servant of God, Well Done!"

God chose a *servant* to be His king over His people. Today in the modern halls of business and power, we usually look for the strongest candidate, the best one on his or her feet at the interview. Who has the most support, the best connections—politically and financially? Who has the most experience, the best public record? Who shares our values or fights for our favorite cause?

That's how people choose leaders, but God selects His leaders differently. He sees the heart and looks for humility, for a servant attitude.

That's pretty much all God requires of His leaders: a humble heart, like the one in young David, the shepherd. The Lord promoted David from the dirty, lowly, isolated life of a shepherd to the most powerful seat in His kingdom.

I can only conclude: Those counting on their superhero strengths need not apply. God's own hand takes care of any opposition. And that's the kind of support I need in this daily battle of living the Christian life. Most of all, it's the kind of humility I need while I serve where I am now, to the glory of the Lord.

Father, You know my tendency to assert my strengths and try to engineer my circumstances. Please give me a sense of balance in these things—an appropriate strength under the control of Your Holy Spirit; that is: humility. In Jesus' name, amen.

He Remains True

I will not violate my covenant or alter what my lips have uttered (Psalm 89:34).

Scripture: Psalm 89:26-34
Song: "There's a Wideness in God's Mercy"

Ever make a deal with your family or friends that you just couldn't keep? In an attempt to lose weight recently, I agreed to either lose a certain number of pounds by a certain date or pay big bucks to my husband and two sons. They also set personal goals and dates.

We all shook hands on the deal and agreed to hold each other accountable—no matter what! Well, as the end date came closer, each of us feared we would not reach our goals. We tried to renegotiate, either for more time or to avoid paying at all. Finally, after much stress on our relationships, we all agreed to call off the deal (and vowed never to do *that* again).

We all had good intentions, but in the end, we just couldn't reach our goals . . . and we also couldn't afford to pay up. Thankfully, when God makes a covenant with us, He not only keeps His Word, but He also forgives us when we fail to keep up our part. That forgiveness was won for us at the cross.

Of course, there are temporal consequences to David's descendents who "do not follow [God's] statues" (v. 30). Punishment came to Israel, but the Lord never took away His love and mercy. He faithfully kept His covenant completely through the work of His Son, Jesus.

I praise You, **Father,** for Your unfailing faithfulness—and for the price of my forgiveness paid by Jesus. I rely on Your grace today in all things. Through Christ, amen.

Thanks, in the Tough Times

How great you are, Sovereign LORD! There is no one like you, and there is no God but you, as we have heard with our own ears. . . . and with your blessing the house of your servant will be blessed forever (2 Samuel 7:22, 29).

Scripture: 2 Samuel 7:18-29
Song: "God Is So Good"

David, the man who composed many great songs of thanksgiving as psalms, leaves us another example here in 2 Samuel. His passionate prayer of thanks and praise to God for His goodness in the present, past, and future would make a glorious hymn today.

You might think that he prayed these words in a moment of joy, feeling full with happiness. No, David speaks this prayer after experiencing great disappointment: God would not allow him to build the temple. Instead, that coveted honor would go to David's son, Solomon.

When I experience the deep hurt of true disappointment, I naturally respond in anger as I express my feelings to God and those around me. But David showed just how humble he was, even as king. He thanked God and pleaded the case for God's faithfulness in keeping His Word.

In other words, he blessed God instead of turning his back in angry defeat. What an example for me, as I experience impatience with God's plans or even disappointment in His apparent lack of care.

Lord God in Heaven, I know You care about every detail and problem in my life. Help me to know and feel Your love today! I pray in the name of Jesus. Amen.

Seeking Sincerely?

Again the LORD spoke to Ahaz, "Ask the LORD your God for a sign, whether in the deepest depths or in the highest heights." But Ahaz said, "I will not ask; I will not put the LORD to the test" (Isaiah 7:10-12).

Scripture: Isaiah 7:10-15
Song: "Prayer Is the Soul's Sincere Desire"

Recently, while praying for God's guidance about a potential new job and move, I asked that God be very clear to me in His answer. No, I didn't ask for a "sign," but I knew I wouldn't mind receiving direction from His Word.

Sure enough, I began to notice certain Bible verses that said things like: "keep doing what you have been doing" and "be content where you are." Well, that was not the answer I wanted, so I held out hope until I got the final word in a phone call, "No. You're not going anywhere right now."

King Ahaz had other plans too. That's why he wasn't open to asking God for a sign—he wouldn't follow God's plan anyway. But he didn't want to admit it to Isaiah, so he piously said, "I will not put the Lord to the test."

He really didn't want to know God's plan for him or for the future of Israel. That's when Isaiah made things very clear, and God gave him a sign for all to see and recognize: the virgin birth of Immanuel, God with us.

Almighty and merciful God, sometimes my heart isn't really in it when I pray for Your guidance. I know what I want, and so I try to get You to endorse my plans. Forgive me, Lord! Help me seek Your will in all sincerity. In the name of Jesus, who lives and reigns with You and the Holy Spirit, amen.

Encouragement from a Friend

When Elizabeth heard Mary's greeting, the baby leaped in her womb, and Elizabeth was filled with the Holy Spirit. In a loud voice she exclaimed: "Blessed are you among women, and blessed is the child you will bear!" (Luke 1:41, 42).

Scripture: Luke 1:41-45
Song: "Blest Be the Tie That Binds"

Today we can check news online—"on the go"—with our wireless mobile devices. We can even get directions for avoiding accidents and traffic jams spoken right from our car's dashboard. We can chat back and forth on Instant Messenger.

But back in Mary and Elizabeth's day, news traveled slowly, person to person. Distances between family members kept them apart—except when God sent the message through His Holy Spirit messenger.

I was at a prayer retreat years ago and jotted notes in my journal when the speaker said things that touched my heart. Here is one entry (a poor paraphrase) that still blesses me today: "The Lord raises up among us some marvelous friends to help us along the way. They aren't perfect people, but they have received a large amount of grace that shines as the reflected glory of God. They can love us in a way that our own souls are lighted by God's light." I apply those words to the strong bond between Elizabeth and Mary. They both knew the love and grace of God and, in reflecting that love, they strengthened one another.

Father, I thank You for deep and lasting friendships within the body of Christ. Use me in these relationships to reflect Your love for those I love. And when I need it, may I draw from the love of my friends. In Jesus' name, amen.

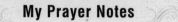

My Prayer Notes